Spotlight on Student Engagement, Motivation, and Achievement

Edited by Caroline T. Chauncey
and Nancy Walser

No. 5 in the *Harvard Education Letter* Spotlight Series

HARVARD EDUCATION PRESS
CAMBRIDGE, MASSACHUSETTS

Library of Congress Control Number 2009927814

Paperback ISBN 978-1-934742-26-6
Library Edition ISBN 978-1-934742-27-3

Published by Harvard Education Press,
an imprint of the Harvard Education Publishing Group

Harvard Education Press
8 Story Street
Cambridge, MA 02138

Cover Design: Don MacDonald

The typefaces used in this book are Humanist 777 for text and
Kuenstler 480 for display.

Contents

Foreword

Sam M. Intrator

I suspect that every teacher who has ever stood before a class clutching a piece of chalk or a marker dreams of routinely striking the sweet spot of practice where students are deeply absorbed in the learning process and exerting intense energy in the task at hand. In these moments, students are focused, concentrating, animated, and eager to persist, even when learning gets difficult.

Conversely, a teacher's worst nightmare involves those classes where heads are down on desks, the air is choked with lassitude, and the environment is raucous with disrespect and resentment. These occasions sap a teacher's morale.

Most teachers know versions of both moments because the work of schooling is complicated, variable, and ever changing. What remains constant for teachers is the understanding that learning and success in school depends on the active engagement of learners. My understanding of engagement traces back to my decision to become a high school teacher. Once I decided to teach, I did what many young people over time have done: I made a pilgrimage to consult with an important mentor in my life. I returned to my old high school in the Coney Island section of Brooklyn and met with Mr. G—a teacher whom I revered during my adolescence.

We met in the library, and after catching up on life, he started to talk me through a stack of lesson plans on teaching poetry, literature, and writing that he had brought. I was fascinated because, as he talked through the sequence of activities in those handwritten pages, I had vague recollections of having participated in, for example, the discussion on Wallace Stevens's poem, "Study of Two Pears," or the activity on Romanticism and creativity. At some point, he paused, peered over the top of his reading glasses, and locked his eyes on me.

"Let me be clear," he said. "Your first and most essential job will be to secure their attention. Your students can't learn if you don't engage them. It begins with engagement." Since that conversation, I have gone on to teach, coach, conduct research, and work as an administrator in many levels of education. Twenty-plus years later, Mr. G's words frame the fundamental question of teaching and learning: What can I do to engage these learners—cognitively, behaviorally, and emotionally so that they put forth the concentrated and purposeful effort necessary for achievement?

This collection of essays provides a bounty of perspectives on this question. It is a survey of thoughtful, inspired, and tenacious initiatives that describe efforts to create conditions where children are actively engaged in the learning process. It asks us to remember that schooling is always a deeply human endeavor replete with joy, triumph, fragility, and risk. I view this volume as important for the following reasons:

- *First, chronic disengagement and boredom are the norm in our schools.* Various studies have found that as children move through their school lives, there is an alarming decline in levels of motivation and academic engagement (McNeely, Nonnemaker, and Blum 2002; Steinberg, Brown, and

Dornbusch 1996). Csikszentmihalyi and Larson's (1984) classic study recording the subjective experiences of children as they move through their day provides an enduring perspective on how children narrate their experiences in school. They find bleak, abysmal patterns of activation, cognitive engagement, and intrinsic motivation: "Compared to other contexts in their lives, time in class is associated with lower-than-average states on nearly every self-report dimension. Most notably, students report feeling sad, irritable and bored; concentration is difficult; they feel self-conscious and strongly wish they were doing something else" (p. 206). Furthermore, classes that are usually considered the linchpin subjects of the school curriculum (English, math, science) rate as the least stimulating.

Disengagement manifests in a range of ways, from apathetic effort on the part of students, to disrespect of the classroom space, to the most visible indication of disengagement: dropping out. In fact, a recent study by the Bill and Melinda Gates Foundation of high school dropouts concluded that the single most critical factor in a youth's decision to drop out was uninteresting classes (Bridgeland, Dilulio, and Morison 2006). In the study's focus groups and interviews, recent dropouts explained that school was "boring, nothing I was interested in," or "it was boring . . . the teacher just stood in front of the room and just talked and didn't really like involve you." A female respondent from Baltimore said, "There wasn't any learning going on," and another complained, "They make you take classes in school that you're never going to use in life."

- *Second, disengagement hurts struggling students the most.* I call this the Ferris Bueller phenomenon. Ferris was the impish, middle-class, suburban adolescent in the 1986 film, *Ferris Bueller's Day Off*, directed by John Hughes. His disdain for all things academic earned him the adulation of his peers. Ferris's disengagement and slacker approach to schooling are understood as a phase or even conscientious resistance to the artificiality of school. The implied message is that, for some, disengagement is almost a rite of passage, with little in the way of enduring or life-shaping consequences. As the National Research Council for the Institute of Medicine (2003) concludes in its report on school engagement,

> When students from advantaged backgrounds become disengaged, they may learn less than they could, but they usually get by or they get second chances; most eventually graduate and move on to other opportunities. In contrast, when students from disadvantaged backgrounds in high-poverty, urban high schools become disengaged, they are less likely to graduate and consequently face severely limited opportunities. (p. 1)

The statistics are sobering: only about half of Latino, black, and Native American students graduate from high school. Being bored in ways that lead to cognitive, emotional, and behavioral disengagement, it appears, costs more to those who can afford it least.

- *Third, MTV trumps the ABCs.* Today's youth are unabashed and savvy consumers of many things. The kids that show up in our classrooms and youth programs have come of age in a milieu in which they have enormous capacity to customize and control the stimuli that reach them. They have thousands of songs to choose from on their iPods, hundreds of stations to surf on their cable, nearly infinite pathways to pursue on the Internet, and absorbing and highly stimulating contexts to explore through video-gaming systems. They know how to point and click, build vast and complex social networks, and fundamentally shape their attentional environment.

It's hard to imagine a young person connected to this highly stimulating world being engrossed by conventional school tasks instead of the fluid and customizable environs that they control. Elissa Moses (2000), a marketing executive who has written extensively about youth culture and the ubiquitous appetite for endless sensation, comments:

> Global teens have been brought up to experience and to expect sensory stimulation. This generation is constantly looking for new thrills that entertain. The preferred music is loud. The movies enjoyed feature fast action. The dances are rhythmic and frenetic. These teens are energy in motion. The craving for new sensations leads these teens to test their mettle and push to the extremes . . . Global teens have very low threshold for boredom, and this is an essential finding for marketers: *Do not bore this generation or it will abandon you.*

If boredom is the enemy of engagement, we must contend with these social, cultural, and technological forces.

• *Fourth, teaching matters most.* In synthesizing the research base on what shapes children's school engagement and motivation to learn, the National Research Council Institute of Medicine (2003) concludes that "although policies at the school level and beyond affect what goes on in classrooms, classroom instruction—how and what teachers teach—is the proximal and most powerful factor in student engagement and learning" (p. 60). It recommends a range of instructional strategies focused on developing higher-order thinking skills, authentic tasks, and the quality of feedback. It also emphasizes that, beyond pedagogical technique, what matters is the quality of relationship between adult and young person.

Children yearn for affirmation, acceptance, and support from the adults who work with them in the classroom setting. In Wilson and Corbett's (2001) study of urban middle school students, the authors conclude that students evaluate teachers on the basis of how caring they perceive that teacher to be. They define caring as "acting in the best interests of others" and suggest that students intuitively understand which teachers demonstrate their caring by holding students to high standards and by "refusing to allow them [students] to fail" (p. 89). They conclude, "It was the quality of the relationships in the classrooms that determined the educational value of the setting" (p. 122).

• *Last, let's add student engagement to our spreadsheets.* When I was an administrator in California, the community where I worked had two high schools. One day a parent who was moving to the district scheduled a meeting with me to talk about which school she should have her daughter attend. She strode in and handed me a folder of spreadsheets and graphs that a real estate agent had given her that compared the two schools. The comparisons were based on test scores. She began by saying, "We're trying to decide which school is better, and based on all the information we have, this school is better." Her glib determination of quality was based on a statistically insignificant two-point differential in average SAT scores.

My response was to invite her to seek out other data. Look in classrooms, walk the hallways, speak to students, sit in on classes, come to our athletic events, attend our drama performances, or stop by the office that arranges community service placements. Look, listen, and consider the way we live together and share our daily existence and interactions within this school. In a sense, I was pleading with her to take into account the quality of the nitty-gritty, everyday interactions that are the essence and soul of a human organization like a school.

I'd like to highlight an initiative pioneered in New York City that surveys students, parents, and teachers about the quality of engagement. Each middle school and high school student fills out a survey that explores a range of variables associated with school success, including the following questions on engagement[1]:

> How much do you agree or disagree with the following statements about your teachers?
>
> Strongly Agree, Agree, Disagree, Strongly Disagree, Don't Know
>
> - My teachers enjoy the subjects they teach.
> - My teachers inspire me to learn.
> - My teachers give me extra help when I need it.
> - My teachers connect what I am learning to life outside of the classroom.

The instrument used to measure engagement may not be flawless; however, it does provide a view that can be used to advance the conversation.

In sum, Reed Larson (2000), the psychologist who has done such important work on positive youth development, contends that the central question for educators is how to get children's fires lit so that they can put forth a conscious and purposeful effort. The essays in this volume provide us with a range of illuminating perspectives that enable us to understand why and how to stoke the fires of engagement.

NOTE

1. See http://schools.nyc.gov/Accountability/SchoolReports/default.htm

REFERENCES

J. M. Bridgeland, J. Dilulio, and K. Morison. *The silent epidemic: Perspectives of high school dropouts*. Washington, DC: Bill & Melinda Gates Foundation, 2006.

M. Csikszentmihalyi and R. Larson. *Being adolescent: Conflict and growth in the teenage years*. New York: Basic Books, 1984.

R. W. Larson. "Toward a psychology of positive youth development." *American Psychologist* 55, no. 1 (2003): 170–183.

C. A. McNeely, J. M. Nonnemaker, and R. W. Blum. "Promoting school connectedness: Evidence from the national longitudinal study of adolescent health." *Journal of School Health* 72, no. 4 (2002): 138.

E. Moses. *The $100 billion allowance: Accessing the global teen market*. New York: John Wiley, 2000.

National Research Council Institute of Medicine. *Engaging schools: Fostering high school students' motivation to learn*. Washington, DC: National Academies Press, 2003.

L. D. Steinberg, B. B. Brown, and S. M. Dornbusch. *Beyond the classroom: Why school reform has failed and what parents need to do*. New York: Simon & Schuster, 1996.

B. L. Wilson and H. D. Corbett. *Listening to urban kids: School reform and the teachers they want*. Albany: State University of New York Press, 2001.

Introduction

Caroline T. Chauncey and Nancy Walser

"Nobody stays in school because of Algebra 2." This remark by educator Rachel Poliner captures much of what this slim volume is about. We live in a time when the comparative benefits—economic and otherwise—of completing high school and going on to college are greater than perhaps at any time in our country's history. The gap between the earnings of those who leave high school without a diploma and those who complete or continue past their high school education continues to widen. Yet nationally our high school graduation rate barely tops 70 percent. Among black and Latino students, and in urban schools, the rate is substantially lower. Young people are coming of age in a society that requires sophisticated thinking, the mastery of complex skills, and in many cases advanced knowledge. They may well need Algebra 2! Yet what keeps students in school—or fails to—is rarely the content that they are taught. It is a peculiar mix of factors—relationships, recognition, and relevance, among others—that creates a climate in which students feel engaged both socially and academically and that lays the groundwork to motivate achievement.

In recent years, the *Harvard Education Letter* has paid increasing attention to the interrelated issues of student engagement, motivation, and achievement. This volume, the fifth anthology in the *Harvard Education Letter* Spotlight series, brings together 15 seminal articles that examine various facets of this topic. What does research tell us about the factors that contribute to student engagement? What do we know about motivation as it pertains to education? What kinds of skills are students most likely to need in the 21st century, and what kinds of pedagogy can support achievement in those areas? Most important, what are schools doing that makes a difference in terms of student engagement, motivation, and achievement, and what can we learn from their innovations?

The book is divided into three sections. The first, "Connecting Engagement, Motivation, and Achievement," looks at ways that schools and teachers can help strengthen the ties among these three factors. The opening chapter, "'R' Is for Resilience," by Nancy Walser, focuses on the "positive attributes, experiences, and attitudes" that are essential to children's success in school and in life. The emphasis on the positive is intentional. A growing body of research shows that schools can play a significant role in fostering resilience, and that nurturing healthy social and emotional development is critical to student achievement. The chapter includes tools and strategies that schools are using to help children acquire the "developmental assets" they need.

Many schools are turning to the use of questionnaires designed to assess student engagement. Chapter 2, "Answers and Questions," by Laura Pappano, examines the use of surveys to understand what school looks like from the students' point of view. Implicit in this approach is the understanding that the risk factors that predict disengagement may have less to do with the student and more to do with the school. The importance of listening to what our students tell us—and responding thoughtfully to their feedback—is at the core of this approach.

On a more intimate level, many schools have introduced advisory programs to ensure that every student is known well by at least one adult, to offer academic support, and to strengthen the connections between home and school. Chapter 3 ("Getting Advisory Right," by Mitch Bogen) details the challenges to implementing successful advisory programs—including teacher resistance, lack of clear purpose, and poor preparation. It examines the research in support of advisories and profiles three successful programs, each tailored to the needs of its particular school.

Chapters 4 and 5 address the connections between student identity and academic achievement. In "How Racial Identity Affects School Performance," former Harvard professor Pedro Noguera chronicles the trajectory of his son's development as a high school student "trying to figure out what it meant to be a young Black man" and discusses recent research on how our society's highly charged awareness of race can affect teachers' perceptions of students and students' perceptions of themselves. In the interview that follows ("Educators As 'Applied Developmentalists'"), Michael Nakkula and Eric Toshalis underscore the urgency of identity development as a key task of adolescence and suggest ways that educators can "channel adolescents' urge to challenge themselves" to create an academic environment that is relevant, motivating, and engaging.

TEACHING FOR ENGAGEMENT

The second section of the book, "Teaching for Engagement," explores the connections among engagement, motivation, and classroom practice. The opening chapter, "Developmentally Appropriate Practice in the Age of Testing," by David McKay Wilson, gives voice to an emerging chorus of concern over the impact of accountability testing on the preK–3rd grade curriculum. It documents several recent reports that recommend extending the "developmentally appropriate" approaches commonly found in preschool classrooms up through kindergarten and the early elementary years, and cautions that disengagement as early as second grade—often the result of inappropriate teaching practice—can predict a student's likelihood of dropping out.

Chapter 7, "Teaching 21st Century Skills," by Nancy Walser, echoes the backlash against an "information-based" curriculum driven by content standards and the demands of statewide accountability tests. A growing number of states have begun to develop curriculum and assessment tools based on skills like creative problem solving, collaboration, and adept use of technology, all of which "are vital to working and living in an increasingly complex, rapidly changing global society." The chapter offers examples of what a 21st century approach looks like in practice.

The advent of new technology is transforming the world inside the classroom, too. Chapter 8, "Better Teaching with Web Tools," by Colleen Gillard, examines how the use of blogs, wikis, and podcasts "propels teachers from lecturing at the front of the classroom to coaching from the back" and offers practical guidance for developing Web-based projects that engage and motivate students.

The next three chapters take a closer look at the issue of motivation. In chapter 9, "The Classroom of Popular Culture," James Paul Gee deftly analyzes how video games make children *want* to learn—for instance, by giving them a sense of agency, ownership, and control and by creating a "cycle of mastery" that always pushes them to the next level of competence—and asks how we can make the experience of learning "as motivating, stimulating, collaborative, and rewarding" as that of playing a well-designed video game.

Chapter 10, "Money and Motivation," by David McKay Wilson, examines the recent wave of policy initiatives offering students financial rewards for good grades or good behavior. It weighs the research evidence on the effectiveness of intrinsic vs. extrinsic rewards, and offers counterexamples of successful programs that seek to motivate students by cultivating their sense of their own efficacy.

In chapter 11, "'Manga Is My Life,'" Michael Bitz describes the transformation that takes place among a group of struggling high school students in an afterschool comics club. Their passion for manga—Japanese comic books—leads to a fascination with Japanese culture and a desire to create comic books of their own. Looking at the persistence, enthusiasm, creativity, and results engendered by this process, he asks poignantly why the club members, so excited about words and language, had to wait until school ended and their regular English and social studies classes were over to explore the world of authorship.

REACHING BEYOND THE CLASSROOM

Stepping back from the classroom, educators also face the challenges of creating a school climate that supports engagement, motivation, and achievement. In chapter 12, "The 'Quiet' Troubles of Low-Income Children," Richard Weissbourd reminds us that many subtle factors may interfere with student engagement and learning—ranging from caretaking responsibilities or switching schools frequently to sleep deprivation or undiagnosed vision problems. He cautions that while schools spend much of their time dealing with "loud" problems like behavior difficulties or drug use, these quiet difficulties all too often slip below a school's radar.

In the attempt to create a safer and more supportive school climate, many schools are looking for more effective and constructive ways of addressing disruptive behavior. Interviewed in chapter 13, "Beyond the Discipline Handbook," George Sugai describes Schoolwide Positive Behavior Supports, a three-tiered framework for helping children cultivate appropriate behaviors—whether in the classroom, the cafeteria, the hallways, or on the bus.

In addition to programs designed to improve school climate, afterschool programs can have a significant impact on student engagement. Chapter 14, "Reinforcement, Richness, and Relationships," by Andreae Downs, looks at the "three Rs" of a comprehensive afterschool program aimed at improving student achievement. The program goes beyond tutoring and homework help to "capture the excitement of learning" through a variety of enrichment activities.

A final, critical link in the chain of engagement, motivation, and achievement is the relationship between home and school. Chapter 15, "Meeting of the Minds," by Laura Pappano, profiles effective approaches for communicating with students' families and suggests ways to lay the groundwork for productive parent-teacher conversations.

Taken together, these articles are intended to provide a useful resource for teachers and administrators who devote themselves to the work of preparing children and young adults for the complex challenges, joys, and responsibilities of adulthood, citizenship, and work.

We would like to thank our colleagues at Harvard Education Press for their ongoing support and in particular to acknowledge with appreciation the assistance of HEP editorial intern Katrina Swartz in preparing the manuscript.

PART I

Connecting Engagement, Motivation, and Achievement

CHAPTER 1

"R" Is for Resilience

**Schools turn to "asset development"
to build on students' strengths**

Nancy Walser

Imagine a teenager as a balloon. One minute it's soaring; the next it's floating toward the ground, heading for a crash. But suppose there's an adult standing nearby who is willing to reach out and give it a gentle bop to send it soaring again? Better yet, what if there are five adults standing in a circle holding a thick web made of yarn? The tighter the web, the less likely the balloon can slip through and hit the ground.

This web-of-yarn exercise was invented by Derek Peterson, an educational consultant and one-man crusader who travels the globe preaching the benefits of youth development to teachers, administrators, school board members, and community leaders. The web—he likens it to a Lakota "dreamcatcher"—is meant to demonstrate the impact of adult intervention in supporting resilience among teens.

Rather than focus on negative behaviors like acting out, drinking, or doing drugs, Peterson and others in the field of youth development are educating adults about "protective factors" and "developmental assets"—the positive attributes, experiences, and attitudes that 30 years of research shows are essential to children's success in school and in life. And they are finding a growing audience, both among administrators who are searching for new ways to motivate and engage teens and among test-weary staffers eager for the pendulum to swing back to a focus on the whole child.

A resurgence of interest in healthy social and emotional development can be seen across the country: from the state of Illinois, which enacted grade-level learning standards for social and emotional development in 2004, to Colorado, which has a statewide youth-development office called Assets for Colorado Youth, and up to Alaska, where the Association of Alaska School Boards has been working with school districts and other organizations since 1995 to get adults more involved in schoolchildren's everyday lives. Through student surveys, focus groups, "relationship plans," and other activities, school personnel are looking for ways to lay the groundwork for a lifetime of achievement and success.

BEYOND RISK PREVENTION

It wasn't so long ago that resilience—the ability to rise above adversity and thrive—was thought to be something a person was just born with. But recent research, including developmental psychologist Emmy Werner's longitudinal study of 698 Hawaiian children born in 1955, has identified key factors that resilient individuals have in common. In contrast to the risk-prevention approach, which concentrates on identifying "at-risk" youth and teaching them to avoid negative behaviors, asset development accentuates positive traits, behaviors, and attitudes and seeks to build on those.

At the forefront of this movement is the nonprofit Minneapolis-based Search Institute, where researchers Peter Benson and Peter Scales have combed through decades of research on resiliency, prevention, and adolescent development to identify 40 positive "assets" and arrange them in a user-friendly framework. Schools and other community organizations can use the framework to measure the collective strengths of their students and see how well these institutions support student resiliency.

Half of these factors are external, such as whether or not a child gets support from family members and three or more unrelated adults, while half are internal, such as whether or not a student cares about school and is motivated to do well. The assets are broadly grouped into eight categories: those that contribute to student support, empowerment, boundaries and expectations, constructive use of time, commitment to learning, positive values, social competencies, and positive identity.

Since 1996, the Search Institute has surveyed 3 million students in grades 6–12 across the country and found a direct correlation between the number of assets a student has and "thriving behaviors," such as getting mostly As on report cards or exhibiting leadership skills. The more assets a teenager has, the less likely he or she is to participate in high-risk behaviors, such as substance abuse, sex, and violence. These correlations are consistent for adolescents regardless of race, ethnicity, gender, age, socioeconomic background, community size, or region, according to the researchers.

More importantly, nearly all of these assets, if missing from a child's life, can be "built through concerted effort by schools and communities," according to Benson. He has identified 22 assets that schools can influence directly (see "Asset Checklist").

"We have always known that human development is inextricably linked with academic development," Benson says, "but in a time in history where we are putting so much emphasis on testing and academic achievement, we risk losing sight of something that is very obvious: Achievement is as much about student development as it is about rigor and curriculum."

ASSET CHECKLIST

The Search Institute has identified 22 assets that schools can influence to help their students become more resilient. How well do you think your school supports each of these?

☐ **Other adult relationships.** Young person receives support from three or more nonparent adults.

☐ **Caring student climate.** School provides a caring, encouraging environment.

☐ **Parent involvement in schooling.** Parents are actively involved in helping young person succeed in school.

☐ **Community values youth.** Young person perceives that adults in the community value youth.

☐ **Youth as resources.** Young people are given useful roles in the community.

☐ **Service to others.** Young person serves in the community one hour or more per week.

☐ **Safety.** Young person feels safe at home, at school, and in neighborhood.

☐ **School boundaries.** School provides clear rules and consequences.

☐ **Adult role models.** Parent(s) and other adults model positive, responsible behavior.

☐ **Positive peer influence.** Young person's best friends model responsible behavior.

☐ **High expectations.** Both parent(s) and teachers encourage the young person to do well.

☐ **Creative activities.** Young person spends three or more hours per week in lessons or practice in music, theater, or other arts.

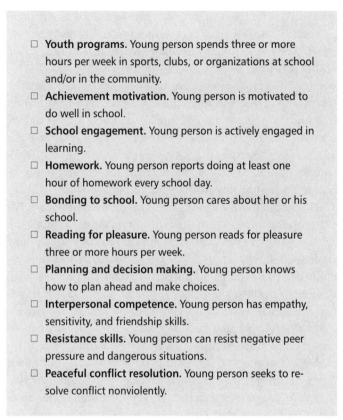

☐ **Youth programs.** Young person spends three or more hours per week in sports, clubs, or organizations at school and/or in the community.

☐ **Achievement motivation.** Young person is motivated to do well in school.

☐ **School engagement.** Young person is actively engaged in learning.

☐ **Homework.** Young person reports doing at least one hour of homework every school day.

☐ **Bonding to school.** Young person cares about her or his school.

☐ **Reading for pleasure.** Young person reads for pleasure three or more hours per week.

☐ **Planning and decision making.** Young person knows how to plan ahead and make choices.

☐ **Interpersonal competence.** Young person has empathy, sensitivity, and friendship skills.

☐ **Resistance skills.** Young person can resist negative peer pressure and dangerous situations.

☐ **Peaceful conflict resolution.** Young person seeks to resolve conflict nonviolently.

Communities that have been successful in building assets among youth are usually those where leaders like the school superintendent, the mayor, or the Chamber of Commerce president "use the bully pulpit to get it going," says Benson.

While the institute pushes asset-building initiatives that target community leaders as the most effective approach to building resiliency, the approach is also popular in schools.

Sixty percent of the nearly 50,000 people trained by the organization in the last two years were school personnel, according to Mary Ackerman, director of external relations at the Search Institute.

Clay Roberts, a senior consultant who has trained administrators and teachers in more than 100 districts for the Search Institute, is seeing more and more Title I and Title II money going to training in asset development. "They really see the link between assets and achievement," he says. Asset development, he adds, is a tool for "engaging those who need to be engaged, whose scores are dragging everyone down."

The Search Institute works with schools in several ways. For example, it contracts with them to administer a 157-question student survey to determine the current level of assets among students, followed up by focus groups to clarify the survey's findings. It also trains administrators and staff in asset development; sponsors a listserv for more than 600 communities engaged in asset work; and hosts an annual conference to share strategies that have worked. Schools usually choose one or more assets to work on, using strategies that may include fund-raising and community service projects; individual "strength interviews," in which advisors help students assess their own assets; or monthly relationship-building campaigns featuring banners that read: "Have lunch with me and find out who I am." Follow-up surveys help school personnel measure progress.

At the heart of this work is the effort to connect children with adults, says Ackerman. "Gates has his R for rigor; ours is for relationships. This is about adults changing so they can be more empowering for kids."

BUILDING ASSETS IN ALASKA

In Alaska, the school board association adopted the asset-development approach in a big way, funneling $2 million per year in funds designated for Native American achievement through No Child Left Behind to school districts and other organizations over a seven-year period for asset-building activities. As the director of child and youth advocacy for the association, Peterson co-wrote a book, *Helping Kids Succeed—Alaskan Style*, which lists concrete ways that families, schools, and religious, tribal, and community organizations can help children develop each of the 40 assets.

While the results are difficult to measure, in Anchorage, the state's largest district, SAT scores are rising steadily, 17 of 21 Title I schools made AYP last year, and drug use is down compared to the national average. "There are a lot of good things to point to," says Sally Rue, director of the Alaska Initiative for Community Engagement at the Association of Alaska School Boards.

Principal Darrell Vincek of the Willard L. Bowman Elementary School in Anchorage in-fuses asset-building into almost everything the school does. Every year at Bowman, staffers participate in "silent mentoring," an activity that begins with writing the name of every student on a paper star and posting it on "The Wall of Stars." Staffers then post their own names on stickies next to the name of any child with whom they have a significant relationship—someone they connect with on a regular basis or who could be counted on to come to them with a problem.

"What we found," says Vincek, "is that some kids have lots of adults in their lives, and there are kids in our building that nobody has a relationship with. Nobody!" Every staff member volunteers to check in with one or two of these students by striking up a casual conversation periodically.

Students are also asked to write a letter every quarter to one significant adult at Bowman to thank that adult for "being a presence in their lives." Students deliver the letters to recipients, and copies are posted in the hallways. Staffers who get letters are often in tears, while those who don't get any or get only a few—well, it's a chance for a little self-reflection, says Vincek.

In a 2005 survey, 35 percent of Bowman students strongly agreed that "adults in my community support this school," compared with 15 percent districtwide. Forty percent strongly agreed that "there is at least one adult at this school whom I feel comfortable talking to about things that are bothering me," compared with 27 percent districtwide.

"We know if kids are connected to schools, they are going to do better, they are going to get their homework in," says Vincek. "These things don't take a lot of time."

ENGAGEMENT LEVELS, RELATIONSHIP PLANS

At the Search Institute, it's Roberts's job to train administrators and teachers how to do things differently in the time they have with students. It's not as easy as it sounds.

Based on his observations, Roberts classified six levels of ability among teachers to engage their students, ranging from the simple "Good morning, how are you?" to higher levels of involvement that give teachers the leverage to influence achievement and other good outcomes for kids. He encourages teachers to take a personal interest in each student, to find out their interests and aspirations, strengths, and talents. The most advanced teachers keep in touch with students over time, he says.

Roberts also works with teachers to make "relationship plans" in addition to regular lesson plans in order to identify potential barriers to connecting with certain students. "You need to get close, very close to those who you think will be the most difficult right away," he advises, "because when you need to discipline them—and you will—they will think you're doing it because you like them. The tendency is to do the opposite."

One reason why educators could be reluctant to get closer to students is explained by a call one Alaska superintendent received from a former student in South Dakota. The student had tracked the superintendent down at his new job in a district on a small island in Alaska to tell him that the student's brother had died. At the end of the conversation, the young man asked, "When are you coming back?"

"There are wonderful, wonderful highs with this work, but it can also be painful," the superintendent notes.

Meanwhile, Peterson continues weaving his web in Arizona, where the state school board association is working on a youth development project similar to Alaska's. "What I am trying to do is create space for very busy people to remember the basic principles of child and youth development," says Peterson. "This is a common sense–based framework with measurable outcomes so that people can come together with common goals for behavior that we'd like to see in classrooms, families, and communities."

This chapter originally appeared in the September/October 2006 issue of the Harvard Education Letter.

FOR FURTHER INFORMATION

B. Benard. *Resiliency: What We Have Learned*. San Francisco, CA: WestEd, 2004.

P. Benson. *All Kids Are Our Kids: What Communities Must Do to Raise Caring and Responsible Children and Adolescents*. San Francisco, CA: Jossey-Bass, 2006.

Initiative for Community Engagement (Alaska ICE), a Statewide Initiative of the Association of Alaska School Boards, 1111 West 9th St., Juneau, AK 99801; tel: (907) 586-1083. www.alaskaice.org

The Search Institute, 615 First Ave. N.E., Suite 125, Minneapolis, MN 55413; tel: (800) 888-7828. www.search-institute.org

N. Starkman, P. Scales, and C. Roberts. *Great Places to Learn: How Asset-Building Schools Help Students Succeed*. Minneapolis, MN: Search Institute, 1999.

CHAPTER 2

Answers and Questions

Schools survey their students—and grapple with the results

Laura Pappano

The most common open-ended response on the High School Survey of Student Engagement is perhaps the most revealing.

"Many kids say, 'Why are we taking this survey? No one will listen to us,'" says Ethan Yazzie-Mintz, survey director at the Center for Evaluation and Policy at Indiana University, whose 2008 High School Survey of Student Engagement reached 68,000 students in 29 states. Although it may sound like a throwaway line, says Yazzie-Mintz, their comment nails the problem precisely: students don't feel heard.

While principals, teachers, and education policymakers are constantly parsing data on student achievement, there is growing concern that data on student engagement—and other aspects of students' experience—are missing. A significant body of evidence links student engagement to graduation rates and academic success. But while educators may think they are involving students intellectually, socially, and emotionally, students often see it differently.

Large-scale student surveys are fast becoming valuable tools for educators. Access to student perceptions, proponents say, offers better information on everything from how welcoming a school is to how well students understand the nuts and bolts of the college application process.

BORED EVERY DAY

What *do* students think about school? The picture from national surveys is not encouraging.

Yazzie-Mintz says data and his experience working with high schools suggest that about 10 percent of high school students are highly engaged and 15 percent are disengaged. Those in between lack strong connections with teachers and find school work irrelevant or dull. Results from the center's 2007 survey show that two-thirds of students are bored in class every day, and 17 percent are bored in every class.

The My Voice survey designed by the Quaglia Institute for Student Aspirations in Portland, Maine, echoes this sense of disaffection. Administered between the fall of 2006 and the spring of 2008 to 414,243 students in grades 6 through 12 in 32 states, the survey found that just 45 percent of students believe teachers care if they are absent from school (see "Five Things to Ask Your Students").

"It would be wrong to say that no schools have paid attention to what kids have been experiencing," says William Damon, whose book *The Path to Purpose: Helping Our Children Find Their Calling in Life* describes a generation of youth adrift. But, says Damon, director of the Stanford University Center on Adolescence, "too many schools have neglected the motives and feelings and experiences of the students and have relied on that old behaviorist model that you stimulate them and expect a response."

FIVE THINGS TO ASK YOUR STUDENTS

Principals and teachers can learn a lot by asking students in grades 6–12 to respond anonymously to the following five statements, says Russell J. Quaglia, founder of the Quaglia Institute for Student Aspirations.

Teachers care if I am absent from school.

__ Strongly agree __ Agree __ Neutral
__ Disagree __ Strongly disagree

Teachers care about me as an individual.

__ Strongly agree __ Agree __ Neutral
__ Disagree __ Strongly disagree

My classes help me understand what's happening in my everyday life.

__ Strongly agree __ Agree __ Neutral
__ Disagree __ Strongly disagree

I learn new things that are interesting to me at school.

__ Strongly agree __ Agree __ Neutral
__ Disagree __ Strongly disagree

School is preparing me well for my future.

__ Strongly agree __ Agree __ Neutral
__ Disagree __ Strongly disagree

For comparison purposes, the percentages of students who agreed or strongly agreed with each statement on the 2008 My Voice national survey are as follows: (1) 45 percent; (2) 48 percent; (3) 38 percent; (4) 64 percent; (5) 65 percent.

Jeremy D. Finn, professor of education at the University at Buffalo SUNY and an expert on dropouts and student engagement, says surveys can tell schools how well they are connecting with students (or not), but the critical piece is that schools take the students' responses seriously.

In a key 1989 paper, Finn described students' decisions to drop out of school not as a single momentous action but as the culmination of a long path of disengagement from school. Schools must stop looking at what kids are doing—the risk factors or attributes that make them likely to disengage—and look at what the *school* is doing, he says. Does your school make kids feel anonymous? Impose excessively strict discipline? Teach courses that feel irrelevant to students? Fail to support students academically or socially in the classroom? "Surveys," he says, "are ways to find out all of these things."

A RANGE OF INSTRUMENTS

A growing array of surveys is available to give students a voice in their education—and educators insight into students' worlds. These range from homegrown school or district questionnaires to large-scale instruments like the High School Survey of Student Engagement (HSSSE). In 2008, 135 high schools paid to have the HSSSE administered to their students. The 35-question survey may be given once a year or, in some districts, every two or more years. The survey asks concrete questions, such as how many papers students write and how much time they spend on homework, as well as posing more philosophical queries, such as, "Why do you go to school?"

The Tell Them From Me survey designed by The Learning Bar, a Canadian company that has gathered data on 100,000 students in the past three years, can give a school principal continuous feedback—even week to week—on the school climate and other indicators, such as students' sense of belonging and interest in classroom learning over time. (Schools can also opt for a twice-a-year "snapshot.") As with the HSSSE, school officials can compare answers with national responses and with schools that have similar characteristics.

The My Voice survey designed by the Quaglia Institute builds its questions around eight themes the institute believes are critical to student engagement and success, with seven questions on each topic. The themes are "belonging," "heroes," "sense of accomplishment," "fun and excitement," "curiosity and creativity," "spirit of adventure," "leadership and responsibility," and "confidence to take action." The 15-minute survey can be paired with a staff survey to uncover what institute director and founder Russell J. Quaglia describes as a gulf between teachers' and students' perceptions. For example, he says, national survey results show that while 96 percent of teachers say they are excited to work with students, only 56 percent of students believe teachers enjoy working with them. "We are not communicating with kids very well," says Quaglia. "It's almost as if we are in two different worlds."

SURPRISED BY THE ANSWERS

As principal of the Portsmouth Middle School in New Hampshire for the past 27 years, John M. Stokel believes that if kids don't feel cared for and connected, they won't perform well scholastically. A few years ago, he partnered with the nonprofit Quaglia Institute and had students complete the My Voice survey. He also created a faculty committee on student aspirations, which conducted student focus groups to supplement the survey's findings.

The results jumped out at him. Just 57 percent of students said they felt teachers cared about their problems and feelings. Focus groups helped clarify the matter. Even though teachers thought they had showed interest by speaking and relating to students' parents, kids didn't interpret that as concern for them. "The teachers feel like, 'I am talking all the time, I'm talking to the parents,'" says Stokel. "But the kid perceives it in a different way."

This and other results spurred Stokel to create a 30-minute advisory program on Monday mornings. By 2007, the school's results on the My Voice survey in the "belonging" category showed big improvement in student perceptions, including an 11-point bump (from 63 percent to 74 percent) in positive responses to the statement, "School is a welcoming and friendly place."

However, Stokel says the survey also revealed other concerns that are not so easily addressed, including students' negative feelings about the school's offering both standard and advanced math and English beginning in seventh grade. "That seems to hit the kids. They look at it as [if] they are being sorted out after sixth grade," says Stokel. Yet, he says, homogenous versus heterogeneous grouping is "such a political issue" that it will take time to craft a solution.

IF YOU ASK, LISTEN

Surveys, in other words, don't just provide information you want. Sometimes they reveal things that are difficult to hear— or fix. Yet if you ask students for their opinions, survey designers say, there is an obligation to act on them.

"We say, 'If you are not going to do anything about it, you may as well not do the survey,'" says J. Douglas Willms, Canada Research Chair in Human Development at the University of New Brunswick and president of The Learning Bar, whose Tell Them From Me survey recently became available in the United States. Willms says school leaders lose credibility if they don't respond—even if it's just doing the easy things, like fixing broken bolts on bathroom stall doors.

One school in Saskatchewan, he says, reports survey results to students on a large video screen at the front of the school.

The format they use ("We asked you . . . ," "You said . . . ," and "We're doing this . . .") lets students see that their input has an effect on their school environment, he says.

Educators must often stifle the urge to reject negative feedback. "They say, 'The kids are making this up,'" reports Yazzie-Mintz. "That is something to examine. If you are going to give students a perceptions survey, you have to start with, 'I'm going to believe what they say.'"

Yazzie-Mintz recalls one high school in an affluent suburb in the Northeast that had made a major investment in technology. When students reported being bored in class, he says, the principal responded, "The students are lying on this thing. They are just trying to make us look bad." Yet when Yazzie-Mintz looked at students' open-ended comments, he saw that they perceived the new technology not as improving teaching and learning but as image enhancement. "A lot of the responses were, 'This school only cares about its image and only does things to look good to outsiders,'" he says. "The school has a lot of work to do."

Despite concerns that students don't take surveys seriously, survey designers say that is rarely a problem. Because students don't disclose their identities, they are free to be frank. The results, notes one survey creator, "are like an anonymous note going under the principal's door."

INTERPRETING THE DATA

Survey results can be overwhelming. What answers merit a response? Should results be vetted by a data person in every school or district? Or should they be accessible to everyone?

The right answer varies by school, survey—and what you are trying to discover. Some surveys yield results that can be easily benchmarked (e.g., what percentage of students are involved in clubs or sports compared with other schools). And even if only a few people in a district have the skills to analyze data fully, others can still scan the results and act on them, perhaps by making lessons more interactive if the survey shows that students are bored in class. Yazzie-Mintz advises that administrators focus on one or two areas of concern so the results don't feel like yet another set of charts.

As principal of the Langstaff Secondary School in Canada's York District, Peter Milovanovic surveyed students at regular intervals using the Tell Them From Me survey, but admits being confused by the data at first. Initially he gravitated to open-ended responses because they were easiest to grasp. Once he became familiar with the data, he says, it became more obvious how to use it. For example, survey results revealed that students were grappling with dramatically higher rates of depression and anxiety than he or school counselors had thought. This spurred him to expand counseling and outreach throughout the school.

Milovanovic says the survey results also gave him important ammunition for solving some long-standing problems in the cafeteria. He brought student feedback to the food service company, which responded by adding more vegetarian meals, adding lower-priced lunch choices, and even replacing three staff members and a manager who clashed with students.

Other results may require additional data or focus groups to decipher. At the Chesterfield Country Public Schools in Virginia, all sophomores and seniors at the 10 high schools in the county complete the HSSSE every two years. School improvement manager Glen Miller notes that administrators use the results in conjunction with other information—and common sense.

For example, when results showed students were writing fewer papers than their peers in other schools, Miller says, they realized after some discussion that the survey was given before reaching the writing-intense portion of the English curriculum. "We had to look at the data and see what really applied to us," he says.

At the Helen Tyson Middle School in Springdale, Ark., school personnel are focused on helping more students get to college. Each year, they question a sample of 100 students using a survey designed by the PALMS (Postsecondary Access for Latino Middle-Grades Students) program. In 2006, principal Todd Loftin says, 94 out of 100 students in his Hispanic-majority school said they planned to attend college, but only half said they knew how to prepare, including which courses to take in later grades.

These results told Loftin that students needed to grasp not just the goal of getting to college but strategies for achieving it. He brought in counselors from two high schools and several colleges, including the University of Arkansas, to give talks about topics like Advanced Placement courses and financial aid. Some of the talks were given for parents, in Spanish.

"In schools, we adults are used to making all the decisions," says Yazzie-Mintz. Student surveys, he says, require "an ideological shift"—the recognition "that kids are smart, kids have insight, kids can actually help us to do this work [that] we need to do better."

This chapter originally appeared in the November/December 2008 issue of the Harvard Education Letter.

FOR FURTHER READING

W. Damon. The Path to Purpose: *Helping Our Children Find Their Calling in Life*, New York, NY: Free Press, 2008. www.williamdamon.com

J. D. Finn. "Withdrawing from School." *Review of Educational Research* 59, no. 2 (Summer 1989): 117–142.

K. Marquez-Zenkov, J. Harmon, P. van Lier, and M. Marquez-Zenkov. "If They'll Listen to Us about Life, We'll Listen to Them about School:

Seeing City Students' Ideas about 'Quality' Teachers." *Education Action Research* 15, no. 3 (September 2007): 403–415.

High School Survey of Student Engagement, www.indiana.edu/~ceep/hssse/

Quaglia Institute for Student Aspirations, www.qisa.org

Tell Them From Me Survey, www.thelearningbar.com

CHAPTER 3

Getting Advisory Right

**Focus and commitment are keys to
connecting with youth**

Mitch Bogen

I t was a particularly tough parent conference. The mother
of a student who had been suspended begged Richard Esparza, then a first-year principal at Granger High School
in Granger, Wash., to readmit her son so he could get his
diploma. When Esparza looked up the student's record, he
found that after four years of school, the student "only had
six credits to his name." The mother, realizing that her son
would not be eligible to graduate, burst into tears.

"That's when I said, 'OK, we better work on our communication,'" Esparza recalls. "I had this experience in my first year,
and in our second year we started our advisory program."

Schools across the country are looking—or in some cases
looking again—at advisory programs, in which teachers meet
regularly with small groups of students to help them navigate
the challenges of school life as a way to improve graduation
rates, family involvement, and academic performance. According to Joe DiMartino, president of the Center for Secondary
School Redesign, who has developed advisory programs with

schools nationwide, "There are a myriad of possible purposes for advisories." All of them, he says, revolve around one goal: creating connections. "Research shows that when students feel connected to the school, they perform much better," he says.

Granger's results support DiMartino's assertion. In the six years after Esparza instituted the advisory program, from 2000 to 2005, graduation rates at Granger—a largely Hispanic school with more than 80 percent of students qualifying for free or reduced-priced lunch—went from 58.3 percent to 89.5 percent, attendance at parent conferences went from 23 percent to 100 percent, and passing rates on state tests showed dramatic improvement. "Was the advisory system solely responsible?" DiMartino asks. "Certainly not. Did it help? It had to."

A growing body of evidence supports the importance of personalized learning environments and strong relationships with school staff in keeping students engaged in school and motivated to learn. These findings provided much of the impetus behind the small schools movement, in which advisory programs are often a key component, and have inspired many larger schools to launch advisories as well. But the simplicity of the idea belies the challenges involved in implementing it effectively. Although many advisory programs have proven disappointing, even schools that have had problems with advisories are going back to the drawing board to try to get it right.

PURPOSE AND PREPARATION

"More attention is being paid [to advisories] than ever before, and more schools are creating their own applications," says Rachel Poliner, coauthor of *The Advisory Guide: Designing and Implementing Effective Advisory Programs in Secondary Schools*, who has been consulting with schools on advisories for two decades. She attributes this rising interest to a new urgency around dropout rates and other social challenges. And in the face of steadily increasing test pressures, she adds, schools recognize that students need both academic and personal support.

Several states are either mandating student advisors in high schools, like Rhode Island, or embracing reform models featuring advisories, such as the Breaking Ranks II initiative developed by the National Association of Secondary School Principals. Financial incentives have come into play as well. The federal government's Smaller Learning Communities program offers grants to schools that provide personalized attention to students, usually in the form of advisory programs. Denise Wolk, coauthor of *Changing Systems to Personalize Learning: The Power of Advisories*, cautions that schools applying for the grants often treat advisories as just another "deliverable" whose requirements can be satisfied with last-minute implementation. Treating advisory programs as anything less than central to a school's mission, she says, almost guarantees a program's failure.

And fail they do. Larry Rehage and Janice Dreis, who ran the flagship advisory program at New Trier High School in Winnetka, Ill., for more than a decade and who now consult on implementation of advisories nationwide, suggest that as many as 75 percent of schools that launch advisories fail to conduct the necessary "initial investigation" to ensure that programs will be running five years later. Specifically, they say, schools need to lay the proper groundwork by

- ensuring sufficient teacher input and support for an agreed-upon purpose
- training teachers to assume the role of adviser
- communicating to students the mission of the advisory experience

- articulating the precise, desired outcomes
- affirming that advisory work is as important as academic coursework
- soliciting feedback from advisers and advisees for improvement

The failure to fund and support proper preparation, they say, overwhelms schools' "tremendous enthusiasm for the concept of advisories and all the benefits they believe can accrue from them." As a result, teachers often regard the program as simply an added burden.

STRATEGIES FOR SUPPORT

Some educators remain skeptical about advisory programs. Michael Goldstein, founder of the Media and Technology Charter High School (MATCH) in Boston, argues that advisories are "an inefficient way of building relationships with kids." Instead of leading advisories, he says, MATCH teachers "use those two to three hours per week on the phone—calling both students and parents, praising good days in class, calling out students to shape up when needed." Goldstein doesn't question that relationships with caring adults contribute to student success, only that advisory programs are the best way to meet that goal.

Wolk agrees that Goldstein's strategy may make more sense for a school like MATCH, which has only 185 students. But she says that most schools aren't even close to being able to provide this level of support. The typical high school guidance program, according to a recent study by Paul Barton of the Educational Testing Service's Policy Information Center, has one counselor per 300 students. The main thing schools should realize, Wolk says, is that whatever strategy you choose, "you can't do nothing."

Poliner agrees: "Nobody stays in school because of Algebra 2. What are adolescents all about? They are about connections, relationships. So they stay in school because someone is showing they care, or because this is where they feel a sense of belonging.

"High achievement requires high support," she adds. "Advisory is the place where you can actually provide the support." Creating daily or weekly rituals is a key ingredient in a successful advisory, Poliner notes. Teachers don't feel burdened by the need to prepare, she says, and students benefit from the "sense of predictability" that a structured approach provides.

As with any growing experience, she observes, schools struggle with advisories—some a little, some a lot. "But I don't experience many schools saying, 'That was a bad idea, we should just move on to something else,'" she says.

VARIATIONS ON A THEME

Like all school reforms, successful advisories need to be tailored to the individual needs of the schools that implement them. "Every school needs to develop its own," cautions DiMartino. "If you try to copy someone else's advisory [program] in your school, it isn't going to work." The three programs profiled below illustrate the variation in the purposes advisories serve, and in how schools address the challenges of implementation and assessment.

"Just Like Their Very Own Kids": Granger (Wash.) High School

At Granger, every teacher becomes responsible for a heterogeneous group of 20 students, whom they follow throughout high school. "What I've charged my staff with," says principal Esparza, is that "they are going to take care of their 20 kids for four years just like they were their very own kids." In practice, he explains, this means the adviser will be "completely centered" on tracking students' grades, monitoring their attendance, and helping them define their career goals, just as any good parent would do. But, he points out, it also means that when advisers see a student struggling, they "sit down and talk to them and get right down to what's going on."

Granger advisories meet four days per week. Subject-area teachers send progress reports to advisers every other week to help kids stay on track. These responsibilities are "built into the schedule," Esparza notes, to ensure that teachers take their advisory responsibilities seriously.

Advisers also reach out to caregivers, keeping them updated on their child's progress and helping them navigate the school system. Esparza emphasizes that good parent outreach doesn't just happen by itself. Granger gives teachers early release time for professional development "to teach the faculty to work with parents."

Over the years, says Esparza, some teachers have balked at assuming these responsibilities, and many have left, either through retirement or transfer. But most of his teachers understand the fundamental point of advisories. "Kids need someone who believes in them," he says.

Connections and Reflections: Parker Charter High School, Devens, Mass.

Parker Charter High School has had an advisory program "since its conception," says Debbie Osofsky, advisories director at the school. Osofsky credits the long-term success of the program to the fact that the school decided to "really hone" its goals for advisory. Administrators settled on four purposes: academic advising, community service, community conversations, and recreation. Even though each advisory is expected to address all four goals, "every group is different, and different emphasis will be placed [on its purpose] depending on the group you have," Osofsky says. The advisories meet in gender-balanced, diverse groups for approximately three hours per week, with two 30-minute "morning connection" sessions, two 30-minute "afternoon reflection" sessions, and one 60-minute "extended time" session on Wednesdays.

Osofsky emphasizes the importance of ongoing assessment, for which the school uses three primary tools: an "advisory check-in" conducted four times per year, which includes criteria for evaluating student participation; a year-end survey to capture student feedback; and ongoing monitoring tied to professional development support (see "Advisory Check-In for Students").

The Second Time Around: Durango (Colo.) High School

Durango High School started over with its advisory program, which, says principal Greg Spradling, was basically an inflated version of homeroom when he first arrived three years ago—a place to "meet and have fun." In his previous role as the principal of Roswell (N.M.) High School, Spradling and his faculty had faced challenges such as low attendance rates and "higher than normal gang activity." They launched the advisory program to "make a connection with the kids to show them they really had an opportunity to succeed and change their lives if they chose to."

Based on the success of that program—Roswell was named a Breakthrough High School in 2004—Spradling came to Durango a believer in the power of advisories. He immediately began work with a group of teachers to develop a formal advisories curriculum. However, not everyone on the staff shared Spradling's belief, and that's where the trouble began. "We implemented it," he says, "but we didn't have total buy-in from the faculty." So Spradling decided to step back to the beginning and "do it right." The school brought in outside consul-

ADVISORY CHECK-IN FOR STUDENTS

How well are advisories working for students in your school? Here are some questions to ask them.

1. Was your adviser clear about the purposes of advisory?
2. Did your adviser motivate and engage advisees?
3. Did you like the activities you did in advisory? Did you learn from them? Did you see their connection to the advisory's purposes?
4. Did your adviser help the group resolve conflicts and stay on task?
5. Did your adviser listen to students and treat them with care, compassion, and respect?
6. Did your adviser serve as your advocate?
7. Did your adviser meet with you individually during the year to address academic and social concerns as needed?
8. Did your adviser maintain contact with your parent/guardian?
9. How would you assess your own performance, attitude, and behavior in this advisory?

Adapted from D. Osofsky, G. Sinner, and D. Wolk. Changing Systems to Personalize Learning: The Power of Advisories. *Providence, R.I.: The Education Alliance at Brown University, 2003.*

tants to help the faculty define their essential purposes for advisory. They came up with two answers: to provide an adult advocate who can help students "through the maze of high school" and to provide them with the support they need. The program is proceeding as a pilot, meeting just one day per week. The school is using "late-in" professional development time to help teachers learn to be advisers.

Spradling estimates that when he came on board maybe half the teachers would have cared if advisories ended. Now, he says, "I think 75 percent of the faculty would probably not want to quit advisory. Those that actually take the time to invest in the curriculum and work closely with the students have realized the value of relationships."

If there is no one template for successful advisories, is there a common thread running through all this diversity?

"For all schools, the details would be different," Poliner says, "but they would all say, 'We know that there needs to be a [place] that's more about the kid than the course content.'"

This chapter originally appeared in the January/February 2007 issue of the Harvard Education Letter.

FOR FURTHER READING

D. Osofsky, G. Sinner, and D. Wolk. *Changing Systems to Personalize Learning: The Power of Advisories*. Providence, RI: The Education Alliance at Brown University, 2003.

R. A. Poliner and C. M. Lieber. *The Advisory Guide: Designing and Implementing Effective Advisory Programs in Secondary Schools*. Cambridge, MA: Educators for Social Responsibility, 2004.

CHAPTER 4

How Racial Identity Affects School Performance

A Harvard professor connects research on race and schooling to his experiences as a student and father

Pedro A. Noguera

When I am asked to speak or write about the relationship between racial identity and academic performance, I often tell the story of my eldest son, Joaquín. Joaquín did extremely well throughout most of his early schooling. He was an excellent athlete (participating in soccer, basketball, and wrestling), played piano and percussion, and did very well in his classes. My wife and I never heard any complaints about him. In fact, we heard nothing but praise about his behavior from teachers, who referred to him as "courteous," "respectful," and "a leader among his peers." Then suddenly, in the tenth grade, Joaquín's grades took a nosedive. He failed math and science, and for the first time he started getting into trouble at school. At home he was often angry and irritable for no apparent reason.

My wife and I were left asking ourselves, "What's going on with our son? What's behind this sudden change in behavior?" Despite my disappointment and growing frustration,

I tried not to allow his behavior to drive us apart. I started spending more time with him and started listening more intently to what he had to tell me about school and his friends. As I did, several things became clear to me. One was that all of the friends he had grown up with in our neighborhood in South Berkeley, Calif. (one of the poorest areas of the city), were dropping out of school. These were mostly Black, working-class kids who didn't have a lot of support at home or at school and were experiencing academic failure. Even though Joaquín came from a middle-class home with two supportive parents, most of his reference group—that is, the students he was closest to and identified with—did not.

The other thing that was changing for Joaquín was his sense of how he had to present himself when he was out on the streets and in school. As he grew older, Joaquín felt the need to project the image of a tough and angry young Black man. He believed that in order to be respected, he had to carry himself in a manner that was intimidating and even menacing. To behave differently—too nice, gentle, kind, or sincere—meant that he would be vulnerable and preyed upon. I learned that for Joaquín, part of his new persona also involved placing less value on academics and greater emphasis on being cool and hanging out with the right people.

By eleventh grade Joaquín gradually started working out of these behaviors, and by twelfth grade he seemed to snap out of his angry state. He became closer to his family, his grades improved, he rejoined the soccer team, he resumed playing the piano, and he even started producing music. As I reflected on the two years of anger and self-destructiveness that he went through, I came to the conclusion that Joaquín was trying desperately to figure out what it meant to be a young Black man. I realized that, like many Black male adolescents, Joaquín was trapped by stereotypes, and they were pulling him down. During this difficult period, it was very hard for me to help him through this process of identity formation. While he was in the midst of it the only thing I could do was talk to him, listen to him, and try to let him know what it was like for me when I went through adolescence.

As a high school student, I coped with the isolation that came from being one of the few students of color in my advanced classes by working extra hard to prove that I could do as well as or better than my White peers. However, outside of the classroom I also worked hard to prove to my less studious friends that I was cool, or "down" as we would say. For me this meant playing basketball, hanging out, fighting when necessary, and acting like "one of the guys." I felt forced to adopt a split personality: I behaved one way in class, another way with my friends, and yet another way at home.

THE EMERGING AWARENESS OF RACE

Awareness of race and the significance of racial difference often begins in early childhood. We know from psychological research that the development of racial identity is very context dependent, especially in the early years. Children who attend racially diverse schools or reside in racially diverse communities are much more likely to become aware of race at an earlier age than children in more homogeneous settings.[1] Interacting with children from other racial and ethnic backgrounds in a society that has historically treated race as a means of distinguishing groups and individuals often forces young people to develop racial identities early. However, prior to adolescence they still do not usually understand the political and social significance associated with differences in appearance. For young children, being a person with a different skin color may be no more significant than being thin or heavy, tall or short.

In adolescence, the awareness of race and its implications for individual identity become more salient. For many young men and women of color, racial identity development is affected by some of the same factors that influence individual identity development in general. According to Erik Erikson and other theorists of child development, as children enter adolescence, they become extremely conscious of their peers and seek out acceptance from their reference group.[2] They become increasingly aware of themselves as social beings, and their perception of self tends to be highly dependent on acceptance and affirmation by others. For some adolescents, identification with and attachment to peer groups takes on so much importance that it can override other attachments to family, parents, and teachers.

For adolescents in racially integrated schools, racial and ethnic identity also frequently takes on new significance with respect to friendship groups and dating. It is not uncommon in integrated settings for pre-adolescent children to interact and form friendships easily across racial boundaries—if their parents or other adults allow them to do so.[3] However, as young people enter adolescence, such transgressions of racial boundaries can become more problematic. As they become increasingly aware of the significance associated with group differences, they generally become more concerned with how their peers will react to their participation in interracial relationships and they may begin to self-segregate. As they get older, young people also become more aware of the politics associated with race, becoming more cognizant of racial hierarchies and prejudice, even if they cannot articulate what it all means.

THEORIES OF THE IDENTITY/ACHIEVEMENT CONNECTION

For educators, understanding the process through which young people come to see themselves as belonging to particular racial categories is important because it has tremendous bearing on the so-called achievement gap. Throughout the United States, schools are characterized by increasing racial segregation[4] and widespread racial disparities in academic achievement.[5] Despite overwhelming evidence of a strong correlation between race and academic performance, there is considerable confusion among researchers about how and why such a correlation exists.

The scholars whose work has had the greatest influence on these issues are John Ogbu and Signithia Fordham. Both have argued that Black students from all socioeconomic backgrounds develop "oppositional identities" that lead them to view schooling as a form of forced assimilation to White cultural values, and come to equate academic success with "acting White."[6] For these researchers, such perceptions lead to the devaluation of academic pursuits and the adoption of self-defeating behaviors that inhibit possibilities for academic success.

My own research challenges Ogbu and Fordham's "acting White" thesis. While carrying out research among high school students in Northern California, I discovered that some high-achieving minority students are ostracized by their peers, but others learn how to succeed in both worlds by adopting multiple identities (as I did). Still others challenge racial stereotypes and seek to redefine their racial identities by showing that it is possible to do well in school and be proud of who they are.

Claude Steele's work on the effects of racial stereotypes on academic performance helps provide a compelling explanation of the identity-achievement paradox. Through his research on student attitudes toward testing, Steele (twin brother of the more conservative Shelby) has shown that students are highly susceptible to prevailing stereotypes related to intellectual ability.[7] According to Steele, when "stereotype threats" are operative, they lower the confidence of vulnerable students and negatively affect their performance on standardized tests. He also notes that the debilitating effects of stereotypes can extend beyond particular episodes of testing and can have an effect on a student's overall academic performance.

As Steele's research illustrates, in the United States we have deeply embedded stereotypes that connect racial identity to

academic ability, and children become aware of these stereotypes as they grow up in the school context. Simply put, there
are often strong assumptions made that if you're White you'll
do better in school than if you're Black, or if you're Asian
you'll do better in school than if you're Latino. These kinds of
stereotypes affect both teachers' expectations of students and
students' expectations of themselves.

Beyond these stereotypes, the sorting practices that go on
in schools also send important messages to students about the
meaning of racial categories. For example, in many schools,
students in the remedial classes are disproportionately Black
and Brown, and students often draw conclusions about the relationship between race and academic ability based on these
patterns. They might say to themselves, "Well, I guess the
kids in these 'slow' classes are not as smart as those in the
honors classes." They also notice that the students who are
most likely to be punished, suspended, and expelled are the
darker students.

Too often educators assume that, because of the choices
Black students make about such things as whom to socialize with or which classes to take, they are anti-intellectual.[8]
However, the vast majority of Black students I meet express a
strong desire to do well in school. The younger students don't
arrive at school with an anti-intellectual orientation. To the
degree that such an orientation develops, it develops in school,
and from their seeing these patterns and racial hierarchies as
permanent. Because a great deal of this behavior plays out in
schools, educators can do something about it.

WHAT CAN EDUCATORS DO?

First, educators can make sure that students are not segregating
themselves, sitting in racially defined groups in the classroom.
For teachers, this can be as simple as mixing students and as-

signing them seats. Or, if work groups are created, students can be assigned to groups in ways that ensure that students of different backgrounds have an opportunity to work together.

Second, educators can encourage students to pursue things that are not traditionally associated with members of their group. If students of color are encouraged by adults to join the debating team or the science club, to play music in the band, or to enroll in advanced courses, it will be possible for greater numbers to challenge racial norms.

Third, teachers can find ways to incorporate information related to the history and culture of students into the curriculum. This is important in helping students understand what it means to be who they are, an essential aspect of the identity formation process for adolescents.

Finally, an effective teacher who is able to inspire students by getting to know them can do a great deal to overcome anti-academic tendencies. They can do this by getting students to believe in themselves, to work hard and persist, and to dream, plan for the future, and set goals.

For many years to come, race will undoubtedly continue to be a significant source of demarcation within the U.S. population. For many of us it will continue to shape where we live, pray, go to school, and socialize. We cannot simply wish away the existence of race or racism, but we can take steps to lessen the ways in which the categories trap and confine us. As educators who should be committed to helping young people realize their intellectual potential as they make their way toward adulthood, we have a responsibility to help them find ways to expand their notions of identity related to race and, in so doing, help them discover all that they may become.

This chapter originally appeared in the March/April 2003 issue of the Harvard Education Letter. *It is excerpted from* Adolescents at School: Perspectives on Youth, Identity, and Education, *edited by Michael Sadowski (Harvard Education Press, 2003).*

NOTES

1. Beverly Daniel Tatum, "Talking about Race, Learning about Racism: The Application of Racial Identity Development Theory in the Classroom," *Harvard Educational Review* 62, no. 1 (1992): 1–24; William E. Cross, *Shades of Black: Diversity in African American Identity* (Philadelphia: Temple University Press, 1991); Jean S. Phinney, "Ethnic Identity in Adolescents and Adults: Review of Research," *Psychological Bulletin* 108, no. 3 (1991): 499–514.

2. Erik H. Erikson, *Identity: Youth and Crisis* (New York: W.W. Norton, 1968).

3. Barry Troyna and Bruce Carrington, *Education, Racism and Reform* (London: Routledge, 1990).

4. Gary Orfield and Susan Eaton, *Dismantling Desegregation* (New York: New Press, 1996).

5. Belinda Williams, "Closing the Achievement Gap," in Milli Pierce and Deborah L. Stapleton (eds.), *The 21st-Century Principal: Current Issues in Leadership and Policy* (Cambridge, MA: Harvard Education Press, 2003); Pedro Noguera and Antwi Akom, "Disparities Demystified," *The Nation*, June 5, 2000.

6. Signithia Fordham, *Blacked Out: Dilemmas of Race, Identity, and Success at Capital High* (Chicago: University of Chicago Press, 1996); Signithia Fordham and John Ogbu, "Black Students and School Success: Coping with the Burden of Acting White," *Urban Review* 18 (1986): 176–206. Also see other works by Ogbu and Fordham.

7. Claude Steele, "A Threat in the Air: How Stereotypes Shape the Intellectual Identities and Performance of Women and African Americans," *American Psychologist* 52 (June 1997): 613–629.

8. John H. McWhorter, *Losing the Race: Self-Sabotage in Black America* (New York: New Press, 2000); Deborah Meier, *The Power of Their Ideas: Lessons for America from a Small School in Harlem* (Boston: Beacon Press, 1995).

CHAPTER 5

Educators As "Applied Developmentalists"

**An interview with Michael J. Nakkula
and Eric Toshalis**

The authors of Understanding Youth: Adolescent Development for Educators *(Harvard Education Press, 2006) discuss the roles educators can play in fostering young people's growth and development.*

What does it mean to understand youth developmentally?

We often talk about adolescents as having "raging hormones" or emphasize their rebelliousness. Assumptions like these reduce adolescents to a stereotype. To understand youth developmentally, it is important for educators to resist the pathologizing "Teens these days!" rhetoric, and instead look and listen for opportunities to participate in their growth. By becoming familiar with underlying patterns of adolescent development, we can deepen our ability to read youth's actions and expressions and respond to their needs.

In our book, we use case studies to show how teachers and counselors can use their understanding of adolescent development to ask generative questions about identity and meaning, and to give specific assignments that help youth negotiate their relationships with peers and adults. The beauty of this is that it's a two-way street: As we help students in their development, they help us develop as educators. Developmental understanding is really as much about our own development as it is about youth's.

You describe educators as "applied developmentalists." How is this different from the way most of us usually see ourselves? What does it require of us?

By "educators," we mean not only teachers but counselors, social workers, psychologists, administrators, mentors, and parents. All of these roles focus on teaching and learning. For teachers, seeing ourselves as applied developmentalists means promoting development beyond the prescribed curriculum. Over the years, we've heard students talk about teachers who treat them like "real people," who care about more than just grades and homework. This can have a powerful effect on motivation. In one of the cases described in our book, a student named Antwon announces that he is not going to do "the teacher's work" because he feels disrespected by her. Even when students know that they, and not the teacher, will pay the price in the long run, they still hold their ground. It's often a matter of dignity and authenticity for them. Personal success is not worth "selling out" to a teacher they perceive as being disrespectful.

As applied developmentalists, it's our job to understand the value of the teacher-student bond and find ways to strengthen it. This doesn't mean compromising academic goals in order to nurture kids. It's the opposite: This is the best way to push our students to the edge of their capacities, particularly the students who struggle most to find school meaningful. In another case, a counselor goes to bat for a student, Lorena, who is bored and getting into fights after school. Believing in the student's untapped leadership and athletic skills, the counselor negotiates a compromise in which the school drops an expulsion threat in exchange for Lorena's promise to participate in an after-school rowing program. Lorena's grades get better as her self-concept grows from mastering skills in rowing—and from being around college students who inspire her to work harder in preparation for college.

There are many ways educators can work with students to build on their strengths, even with all the pressures to focus solely on content and tests. In fact, these pressures only argue for more emphasis on this kind of relationship building.

Many of the issues young people are exploring are very personal—family relationships, sexuality, racial identity, questions about values and faith. These are awfully sensitive issues for both adults and young people. Isn't it safer to leave them at the classroom door?

The truth is, students never leave those things at the classroom door, nor do educators. They are sensitive issues precisely because they are so critical to who we are. As we say in the book, "Our work in schools is identity work." Our family upbringing, sexual orientation, racial and ethnic identity, and faith perspectives are so fundamental to who we are and how we represent ourselves to others—for youth just as much as for adults. What better way to make schools relevant and engaging than to incorporate these kinds of issues into the way we teach, counsel, and administer? If we only pick "neutral" or "safe" issues to teach in our schools, are we really preparing youth for adulthood?

Excising crucial developmental issues from education is a surefire way to make things boring for students and routine for educators. Our students know what they want to talk about, and it can be frustrating and demoralizing not to have a safe space for these important conversations. In our experience, adolescents are quick to name the favorite educators with whom they can "get real" about the meanings they are discovering in their lives, as contentious and complicated as they may be. Youth are drawn to such people not because they avoid sensitive issues but because they are sensitive enough to address them, thereby providing opportunities for growth. These are usually educators who take risks along with their students, like being honest when things aren't going well in the hope of clearing up misunderstandings, or by honestly assessing a student's strengths and weaknesses in order to provoke a positive change.

How can a developmental perspective change the way we deal with adolescent risk taking?

When we talk about risk taking, let's be careful to distinguish it from being "at risk." Risk taking is a means of exploration; it's a means of pushing ourselves beyond our comfort levels. Unfortunately, risk taking can place adolescents at risk for devastating experiences—addiction, car accidents, violence. Risk taking and experimentation are part of what makes adolescents tick. Developmentally, it is the way they find out who they are in relation to their peers and the world and organize themselves for future pursuits.

As educators, we have a unique opportunity to channel adolescents' urge to challenge themselves. We can create classroom environments that support creative expression and provide spaces for students to create, to experience intensely, to perform. Showing our passion for the subject we teach is one way to model and connect. Role-playing activities, debates, problem-posing assignments, and performance-based assessments are other ways to provide outlets for a teen's natural desire to experiment and "try on" different selves. The fewer such options our students have in school, the more likely it is that they will indulge their risk-taking proclivities elsewhere. Students need adults to be allies in this critical time of identity building. Educators can be what's being called "natural mentors" in this process.

What are some of the most common mistakes teachers and administrators make in dealing with young people?

Working with teenagers can sometimes be disconcerting, to put it mildly. When they challenge us or resist our attempts to educate them, we can feel vulnerable. Sometimes we compensate for this vulnerability by trying too hard to control them. But adolescents rarely respond well to excessive control. In schools where bell schedules, standardized tests, and detentions loom larger in students' lives than connection, inquiry, dialogue, and challenge, developmental opportunities are being lost. Sure, structure and order provide safety and predictability in schools, but if educators make them the ends instead of the means, youth invariably learn to seek growth opportunities outside of and frequently contrary to school.

Just like adults who complain that we don't have enough freedom or creativity in our jobs, adolescents want negotiable relationships and spaces in which they are encouraged to experiment and recognized as capable. They want to work with people who can respond to their cultural distinctiveness, push them to the edge of their capacities, and provide options. As some of our case studies show, when someone breaks a rule or gets in trouble, educators can play a critical role by trying to get to the root of the problem, be it a peer issue or test anxiety, instead of focusing on the infraction only.

By listening developmentally instead of judgmentally, educators can help facilitate a process for students to get back on track—and earn the students' respect along the way. If there is a common mistake educators make in working with adolescents, it is that we forget that the meaning they are making of their lives is theirs, and the best way to participate in developing it may look less like control and more like getting out of the way.

If you could make one change in the way high school teachers and staff relate to their students, what would it be?

More listening, less talking, with an emphasis on possibilities rather than problems.

This chapter originally appeared in the online edition of the January/ February 2007 issue of the Harvard Education Letter.

PART II

Teaching for Engagement

CHAPTER 6

Developmentally Appropriate Practice in the Age of Testing

**New reports outline key principles
for preK–3rd grade**

David McKay Wilson

As the push to teach literacy and math skills reaches farther into preschool and kindergarten, educators are warning that teachers need to address young students' social, emotional, and physical needs as well as their cognitive development. Among their concerns:

- Teachers in preK–3rd grade increasingly focus on a narrow range of literacy and math skills, with studies showing some kindergarteners spend up to six times as much time on those topics and on testing and test prep than they do in free play or "choice time."
- Many schools have eliminated recess or physical education, depriving children of their need to move and develop their bodies.
- Instruction is often focused on "scripted" curricula, giving teachers little opportunity to create lessons in response to students' interests.

• Some state standards for literacy are too stiff, such as one state's standard that all students be able to read by the beginning of first grade.

In light of these concerns, several prominent early childhood organizations have issued reports on the importance of incorporating developmentally appropriate practice into elementary school classrooms, based on what research has confirmed about early learning.

The National Association for the Education of Young Children (NAEYC) is so concerned about the pressure to prepare students for third-grade standardized tests that it adopted a position statement in early 2009 on developmentally appropriate practice for educators in preK through third grade. In their report, "Developmentally Appropriate Practice in Early Childhood Programs: Serving Children from Birth Through Age 8," NAEYC researchers outlined 12 principles of child development that can be incorporated into classroom teaching (see "NAEYC's 12 Principles of Child Development").

The report urges educators to incorporate play into daily instruction, devise classroom tasks that are challenging yet attainable, and become attuned to the needs of each student so that materials can be adapted to a child's individual needs. It also urges educators in preK through third grade to learn from each other: While preschool educators can benefit from understanding the standards children are expected to meet by third grade, NAEYC believes primary-grade teachers can improve the quality of their instruction by learning more about children's developmental needs from early childhood educators.

The Alliance for Childhood's report, "Crisis in Kindergarten: Why Children Need to Play in School," cites nine new studies that focus on the role of play, child-initiated learning, highly structured curricula, and standardized testing. One study found that the preponderance of time in 254 New York

NAEYC'S 12 PRINCIPLES OF CHILD DEVELOPMENT

- All domains of development and learning—physical, social and emotional, and cognitive—are related.
- Children follow well-documented sequences to build knowledge.
- Children develop and learn at varying rates.
- Learning develops from the dynamic interaction of biological maturation and experience.
- Early childhood experiences can have profound effects, and optimal periods exist for certain types of development and learning.
- Development proceeds toward greater complexity and self-regulation.
- Children thrive with secure, consistent relationships with responsive adults.
- Multiple social and cultural contexts influence learning and development.
- Children learn in a variety of ways, so teachers need a range of strategies.
- Play helps develop self-regulation, language, cognition, and social competence.
- Children advance when challenged just beyond their current level of mastery.
- Children's experiences shape their motivation, which in turn affects their learning.

City and Los Angeles kindergartens was spent on literacy and math. Teachers reported that the curricula didn't have room for dramatic play, blocks, or artistic activities, and that school administrators didn't value such activities. A report from the American Academy of Pediatrics, however, concluded that play was essential for healthy brain development. And a cross-national study of 1,500 young children in 10 countries found that children's language at age seven improved when teachers let them choose their activities rather than teaching them in didactic lessons.

"The studies showed that teachers were spending two to three hours a day hammering in their lessons, with little time for play," says Joan Almon, executive director of the Alliance for Childhood. "The brain is eager to learn at this age, but the kids are more eager to learn from things they can touch and feel."

Charging that "developmental psychology and education have grown apart," the FPG Child Development Institute in Chapel Hill, N.C., is also advocating for more professional development and coursework for teachers in the science of child development. The institute's researchers emphasize the importance of four foundations of learning: self-regulation, representation, memory, and attachment (see "Four Foundations of Learning").

"The ability to focus, pay attention, and work with others is very predictive of long-term success in school," says Carol Copple, coeditor of the NAEYC report. "Those things are typically emphasized in preschool, but they are important for older children as well."

RESPONSIVENESS AND ENGAGEMENT

Developmentally appropriate practice is based on the recognition that child development generally occurs in a predictable sequence of stages. While children may develop at different rates, each stage of development lays the groundwork for the acquisition of new skills and abilities in the next phase. Research has long indicated that children do best when they are supported to achieve goals just beyond their current level of mastery.

FOUR FOUNDATIONS OF LEARNING

Teachers of children from preK to age eight should focus as much on self-regulation, representational thought, memory, and attachment as they do on basic skills, say researchers at the University of North Carolina's School of Education.

These four issues serve as the foundation for young children's development, according to Sharon Ritchie, a senior scientist at FPG Child Development Institute and coauthor of the report, "Using Developmental Science to Transform Children's Early School Experiences." She offers the following examples:

- *Self-regulation* is often developed through play. For example, when kindergartners play "restaurant," they must regulate their behavior to stay in the role of customer, waiter, cashier, or store manager. As children grow older, their play follows more complex rules, as when third-graders act out a story they have read.
- Secure *attachment* relationships help young children feel comfortable exploring the world to learn. Teachers can nurture good relationships by helping students express their feelings and resolve conflicts.
- *Representational thought* is the ability to use an expression—be it a word, gesture, or drawing—to depict an idea. Teachers need to help children find ways to express their own ideas before guiding them to new understanding.
- *Memory* is a crucial part of learning. Strategies to help strengthen students' memory include encouraging students to talk about what they have just learned or, as they grow older, reflecting on what they do when they need to remember something. Teachers can also structure their classes to help children remember the most important items taught that day.

In crafting their report, NAEYC researchers reviewed recent educational research, interviewed scores of experts, and observed classrooms. They note the crucial connection between children's social and emotional life and their academic competence. Children make the biggest strides, the authors found, when they are able to cement secure, consistent relationships with responsive adults.

For classroom teachers, they say, being responsive means being able to adapt the curriculum to address their students' needs and interests and to allow children to discuss their experiences, feelings, and ideas. That can be difficult when teachers are following the highly regimented lesson plans now mandated in many classrooms.

Developing an enthusiasm for learning is especially important in the primary grades. Even students who have excelled in preK or kindergarten can find first or second grade so trying that they turn off to learning. Such disengagement has become so widespread that Sharon Ritchie, a senior scientist at FPG Child Development Institute, has worked with educators on a dropout-prevention project that focuses on children in preK through third grade.

"You can walk into a classroom and see kids who by third grade are done with school," she says. "They are angry and feel school is not a fair place or a place that sees them as the individual that they are."

Some of that disengagement, Ritchie says, is rooted in the way students in second or third grade are taught. She found that students in preK classes spent 136 minutes a day involved in hands-on projects. That dropped to 16 minutes by kindergarten and 12 minutes a day by second and third grade.

She encourages teachers to use hands-on activities in kindergarten and the early primary grades to allow students to experience learning through inquiry. In a first-grade lesson on evaporation, for instance, Ritchie suggests that the teacher ask the children to describe where they think rain comes from and have them draw pictures depicting their theories. Based on that information, the children can discuss their hypotheses and begin to investigate what actually happens. For example, they might observe an ice cube at room temperature as it melts and then evaporates. Older children could deepen their inquiry through library research or designing and performing their own experiments.

Teachers also need to listen to what interests their young students. Patricia Lambert, principal of the Barnard Early Childhood Center in New Rochelle, N.Y., says listening to students can spark engaging lessons. At her school, which serves children from preK through second grade, teachers are encouraged to weave district-mandated outcomes into lessons that teach but do not drill. "Our goal by the end of kindergarten is to have children count from zero to 20," she says. If the children are learning about sharks, she adds, "we may use a model of a shark, and count the shark's teeth."

"I'm all for exposing preschool children to numbers and letters," Lambert says, "but we introduce by listening to what the children are interested in and then gently imposing these concepts on their interests."

LEARNING THROUGH PLAY

Young children do much of their learning through play, says Robert Pianta, dean of the Curry School of Education at the University of Virginia, but adults need to guide their play to help them learn. "It's a misinterpretation to think that letting students loose for extended periods of time is going to automatically yield learning gains," he says. "This is particularly true for students struggling to self-regulate and communicate."

Teachers must intentionally engage with their students, shaping play in a way that's enjoyable, while providing the child with the information and skills to allow playful exploration to produce learning. With blocks, for example, a teacher can talk about shapes, sizes, and colors to help the student bring those concepts to life.

That intentional engagement, says Sharon Kagan, the Marx Professor of Early Childhood and Family Policy at Columbia's Teachers College, should be subtle and keyed to a child's particular needs. If a boy is having trouble using scissors, then scissors, paste, and other art supplies should be set up for him at a table. "The teacher shouldn't push the child to the table, but needs to provide encouragement," she says. "Then the teacher can watch and monitor and guide."

Other advocates, however, note that some of the richest learning for children comes through child-initiated or child-directed play. The Alliance for Childhood report recommends at least three daily play periods of an hour or longer in a full-day, six-hour kindergarten program, with at least one hour spent playing outdoors.

LET'S GET PHYSICAL

At a time when some schools are cutting recess and physical education classes in favor of academic instruction, researchers say these districts are depriving children of essential school-based activities that prepare them for learning. The NAEYC report, for example, recommends that children play outside every day, have regular physical education classes, and have ample opportunities to use their large muscles for balancing, running, jumping, and other vigorous activities.

A recent study in *Pediatrics* detailed the benefits of recess for third-graders. Dr. Romina Barros, pediatrician at Albert Einstein College of Medicine in New York City, surveyed about 11,000 eight-year-olds and found that 30 percent had little or no recess. Those who had at least 15 minutes of recess exhibited better classroom behavior than those who didn't have a break.

The study shows that giving children a break from their studies helps them with self-regulation, a key predictor of long-term success in school. On the playground, children learn how to resolve conflicts, control their actions in a game, and take turns. They also get to use some of that natural energy that spills out of some children in the classroom and can be seen as disruptive.

"You can't move forward with another half-hour of math if you see the kids are bouncing out of their skins," says Alice Keane, a first-grade teacher at Lake Bluff Elementary School in Shorewood, Wis. "We might take what we call a 'wiggle walk' around the school because the kids in the class have too many wiggles. It's amazing how more receptive the children are after they've moved around."

This chapter originally appeared in the May/June 2009 issue of the Harvard Education Letter.

FOR FURTHER READING

R. M. Barros, E. J. Silver, and R. E. K. Stein. "School Recess and Group Classroom Behavior." *Pediatrics* 123, no. 2 (2009): 431–436.

J. D. Bransford, A. L. Brown, and R. R. Cocking. *How People Learn: Brain, Mind, Experience, and School.* Washington, DC: National Academy Press, 2000.

K. L. Maxwell, S. Ritchie, S. Bredekamp, and T. Zimmerman. *Issues in PreK–3rd Education: Using Developmental Science to Transform Children's Early School Experiences* (#4). Chapel Hill: University of North Carolina, FPG Child Development Institute, FirstSchool, 2009. Available online at www.fpg.unc.edu

E. Miller and J. Almon. "Crisis in Kindergarten: Why Children Need to Play in School." College Park, MD: Alliance for Childhood, 2009. Available online at www.allianceforchildhood.org

National Association for the Education of Young Children, www.naeyc.org

Teaching Strategies, www.teachingstrategies.com/index.cfm

CHAPTER 7

Teaching 21st Century Skills

What does it look like in practice?

Nancy Walser

Call it a quiet revolution. As 2014 approaches—the deadline for all students to be proficient on state tests—academics, educators, business groups, and policymakers are finding common ground in a movement to bring "21st century skills" to the classroom, prompting state agencies and district leaders across the country to rewrite curriculum standards and even to contemplate big changes to existing state testing systems.

What are 21st century skills, who's pushing them, and what does 21st century teaching look like in practice?

Although definitions vary, most lists of 21st century skills include those needed to make the best use of rapidly changing technologies; the so-called "soft skills" that computers can't provide, like creativity; and those considered vital to working and living in an increasingly complex, rapidly changing global society (see "Skills for a New Century,").

"Some of these skills have always been important but are now taking on another meaning—like collaboration. Now you have to be able to collaborate across the globe with someone

SKILLS FOR A NEW CENTURY

Most lists of 21st century skills include some or all of the following:

Critical thinking
Problem-solving
Collaboration
Written and oral communication
Creativity
Self-direction
Leadership
Adaptability
Responsibility
Global awareness

you might never meet," explains Christopher Dede, a Harvard professor who sits on the Massachusetts 21st Century Skills Task Force. "Some are unique to the 21st century. It's only relatively recently, for example, that you could get two million hits on an [Internet] search and have to filter down to five that you want."

While progressive educators in the past have often been wary of education reforms spearheaded by big business, the outsourcing of menial jobs and the need for workers to compete in a global economy have brought about an unprecedented convergence of interests, argues Tony Wagner, author of *The Global Achievement Gap* and codirector of Harvard University's Change Leadership Group. Surveys of business leaders show that when hiring new employees, they are looking for the same higher-order thinking skills as those considered necessary for students to do well in college, he notes.

Wagner and others also point to signs of student disengagement from traditional forms of learning that value memorization and mastery of content over student-designed demonstrations of skills. They cite surveys indicating that U.S. high schoolers drop out more from boredom than failure.

"Making AYP [adequate yearly progress] is absolutely no guarantee that students will be ready for college, citizenship, and employment," says Wagner, noting the high number of students needing remedial coursework in college—including those who graduate from schools boasting high standardized test scores. "Our curriculum is information-based and the emphasis is to acquire information first and foremost, and secondarily acquire skills," he says. "We have it exactly backwards."

Teaching 21st century skills doesn't necessarily mean using a lot of technology, although projects may involve computers, software, and other devices, like a global positioning system (GPS). Sometimes it's simply a matter of approaching an assignment differently to allow students to demonstrate skills like teamwork, collaboration, and self-directed learning. Equally important is making sure teachers are able to coach students on how to advance to the next level of a particular skill. This is often done with rubrics that explain clearly what poor, average, and effective skills look like in practice.

What follows are some examples of 21st century teaching provided by researchers, curriculum specialists, administrators, and teachers.

Try a Socratic seminar. Instead of relying on the usual lecture-question format, ninth-grade humanities teachers Mark Rubin-Toles and Torie Leinbach, who teach in the Catalina Foothills school district outside Tucson, Ariz., require students to lead their own discussions about a book, documentary, or document they have studied. Students are graded on the quality of their participation. Good marks go to those who build on, clarify, or challenge others' comments while referencing information from the material, their own experience, or other current events, according to a rubric given to them in advance.

"In the beginning, they struggle a lot," says Rubin-Toles, who limits his role to mapping the interactions on paper while the students talk. "There are these long silences and the kids are very uncomfortable." Later in the year, in the best of conversations, the students make connections with material they discussed earlier, he says.

The exercise builds critical thinking, oral communication, flexibility, self-direction, and teamwork. "They have to listen to others to do well," says Rubin-Toles. "Part of teamwork is holding back, especially when you have something to say. It's like a meeting of adults."

Beautify the neighborhood. Sixth-grade science teacher Wayne Naylor has found a way to weave 21st century skills into lessons on longitude and latitude and on scale and proportion—required by Indiana state standards—while also working to get his town certified as a wildlife community by the National Wildlife Federation. In his class at Craig Middle School, students work in groups to identify natural areas in surrounding Lawrence Township that need improvement. One such project was restoring and renovating the city's Fall Creek Park to remove invasive species. Using the Internet, students researched plants native to the area. They conducted surveys to gather ideas from others in the community about their plans. Using a GPS and Google Earth, they marked the locations of their projects and created poster displays and scale models. Some groups went further, producing a videotape to apply for a national Christopher Columbus award, which is given to teams of middle school students who use science and technology to find an innovative solution to a community problem. They followed up by implementing the plans they designed.

Naylor's six-week unit has something to engage everyone, he says. One student with attendance problems never missed Naylor's class. Although the student struggled in math class, when it came to translating proportions from a model picnic table to build the real thing (which now sits in the school courtyard), "he did just fine," says Naylor. "He was a leader. Everyone was really impressed."

Build a bridge. Not everyone has access to 40-foot pine trees, but in rural Darlington, Wisc., high school teacher Dick Anderson sized the opportunity to use local rough-sawn timber to impart some 21st century skills and real-world entrepreneurship to his students.

Each year for the past two years, students in Anderson's elective Building Trades class have been involved with nearly every aspect of planning, budgeting, modeling, building, and siting a rustic covered bridge. Students worked 60 hours outside of school to complete the last one. In a real lesson in adaptability, the plan to site it over the nearby Pecatonica River had to be abandoned due to environmental issues. The plans were scaled down so the bridge would fit in a city park near a new motel.

The project went beyond the typical trades class in which students learn technical skills in isolation from the real world, says Anderson. Students gave numerous presentations to school board members, the city council, and business groups, and even gave interviews to reporters from a local TV station. "They had to convince responsible adults to say, 'Yes, we'll take a bridge for the city of Darlington,'" said Anderson. "They learned that if you want to get anything done, that's the way it is."

Make an I-Movie. Catalina Foothills teacher Dana Mulay and her kindergarten class were getting bored with point-and-click software games. So, to keep her five-year-olds excited about learning, she decided to help them use I-Movies software to create videos featuring the solid shapes they were studying in math. She divided them into teams and, armed with digital cameras, they went into the desert nearby hunting for shapes to photograph. "Barrel cactus sort of look like spheres and a seguero [cactus] is a cylinder," she says. She downloaded the photos on to laptops brought into the class on carts, and students worked in pairs to make the movies, using invented spelling for captions. The project helped them learn more not only about computers, but also about teamwork and self-direction, she says. "It was really amazing to see them problem-solve on their own and focus on what they needed to do."

Save a river. A block and a half away from the seventh most endangered river in the United States sits the Hayes Bilingual Elementary School in Milwaukee. It's where library media specialist Tomas Kelnhofer is using 21st century tools to work with fifth-grade teachers and students—the majority of whom come from Spanish-speaking homes—to learn about science, their community, and their planet. The Kinnickinnic River "has been an eyesore—a drainage ditch and dumping ground," says Kelnhofer. Except for occasional debris floating down the wide, concrete-lined channel, the river was invisible to students. Not any more. Partnering with local health and environmental groups, students have canoed down the river to see places where PCB-laden sediment has collected. They have tested water for bacteria, posted reflections in online journals using Moodle, and created a DVD and Power-Point presentations of their plans to enhance the river area. They have also debated moral dilemmas such as whether the city of Milwaukee should continue to use salt on icy roads for safety, given the impact on wildlife in the river. "It's true that our students are going through a continuous revolving door of assessments, including those required by NCLB," says Kelnhofer. "However, in between these assessment cycles there is

In Arizona, the Catalina Foothills district settled on 12 skills to teach their students and has rewritten its standards and report cards with those in mind.

In 2008, the Virginia Beach, Va., school district completed a year-long strategic planning process that included 250 community members. "The resounding message was, 'Forget the tests, don't worry about the scores, prepare our kids for the world,'" says superintendent James Merrill. As a result, the 72,000-student district is looking at only one strategic goal for the next five years: "By 2015, students will master the skills they need to succeed to be 21st century learners, workers, and citizens."

Others, like Dede, believe that until states adopt better ways to measure 21st century skills, it will be difficult to bring about a shift in classroom priorities.

"You can't just sprinkle 21st century skills on the 20th century doughnut," he says. "It requires a fundamental reconception of what we're doing."

This chapter originally appeared in the September/October 2008 issue of the Harvard Education Letter.

FOR FURTHER READING

Catalina Foothills School District, www.cfsd16.org

Christopher Columbus Awards, www.christophercolumbusawards.com

Darlington, Wisc. High School Timber Framed Covered Bridge Project, www.summerville-novascotia.com/darlingtoncoveredbridge/

C. Dede. *Transforming Education for the 21st Century: New Pedagogies That Help All Students Attain Sophisticated Learning Outcomes.* Available online at www.gse.harvard.edu/~dedech/Dede_21stC-skills_semi-final.pdf

Iowa Core Curriculum and 21st Century Skills, www.iowa.gov/educate/content/view/674/1023

F. Levy and R. Murnane. *The New Division of Labor: How Computers are Creating the Next Job Market*. Princeton, NJ: Princeton University Press, 2005.

The New York Performance Standards Consortium, http://performance-assessment.org

North Carolina Professional Teaching Standards, www.ncptsc.org

Partnership for 21st Century Skills, www.21stcenturyskills.org

T. Wagner. *The Global Achievement Gap*. New York, NY: Basic Books, 2008.

West Virginia Department of Education Teach21, http://wvde.state.wv.us/teach21

Wisconsin 21st Century Skills Initative, www.21stcenturyskills.org/route21/

CHAPTER 8

Better Teaching with Web Tools

How blogs, wikis, and podcasts are changing the classroom

Colleen Gillard

- *Eric Langhorst's eighth-grade American History students in Liberty, Mo., listen to his podcasts about the Boston Tea Party while walking their dogs, doing chores, or getting ready for bed.*
- *Ben Sanoff's World History students in Berkeley, Calif., discuss their essays via instant messages before posting their final drafts to the class blog by midnight deadlines. Later they return to the blog to read and discuss one another's work.*
- *Fifth graders in College Park, Ga., create a wiki so compelling it receives over 1,000 hits from as far away as Indonesia, Turkey, and Latin America in the first few days after it's posted. The site, centered on a historical novel, includes a slide show, maps, historical background, and interviews.*

From blogs to wikis to podcasts, teachers in schools across the country are beginning to use Web tools to enhance student learning. If these tools are transforming how students learn, they're also changing how teachers teach.

Those who have waded into this brave new world say the use of Web tools in the classroom naturally propels teachers from lecturing at the front of the room to coaching from the back, a direction in which education professionals have been trying to steer teachers for decades. With their peers—or the world—as their audience, students are eagerly seizing the opportunity to take charge of their learning.

This is what Debbie Herzig of Woodward Academy in College Park, Ga., says happened when she asked her fifth-grade students to build a wiki—a collaboratively written and edited Web site—around *Turn Homeward, Hannalee*, Patricia Beatty's book about Georgia mill workers during the Civil War. Students started the project with traditional classroom activities, like researching historical facts about the Civil War, creating a dictionary of mill terms, and taking a field trip to the ruins of a period mill. To create their wiki, students brainstormed topics for the Web site representing the important events and themes in the book, such as "Life of a Millworker" and "Civil War Time Line and Map." The students divided into groups to design and build these sections of the wiki, known as "wiki pages," and then critiqued one another's pages, editing for content, spelling, and grammar.

Students were motivated by the idea that their wiki could serve as a resource for other students and teachers on the Internet, according to Herzig. They were also enthusiastic about the opportunity to design their own wiki page and to edit one another's work. Herzig recalls that she and her coteacher had to resist the temptation to jump in and edit the students' work and learn to be comfortable with a "chaotic" process. Nonetheless, the teachers found the students patient and helpful with one another. "You always emphasize editing as an important part of the writing process, which can be a real chore for kids. But in this case, they really got its importance," says Herzig.

GETTING STARTED

Using Web tools comes more naturally to students than teachers, and young people will continue to outstrip adults in their use of these tools, says Will Richardson, a former teacher and author of the popular book *Blogs, Wikis, Podcasts, and Other Powerful Web Tools for the Classroom*. "Kids instant message as if they were using a pencil. They use Facebook and MySpace without even thinking of them as blogs," he says.

For teachers, Web tools can seem fairly disruptive, not merely because they raise safety or privacy concerns, or even because of the technological challenges they present, "but more significantly because they demand a whole new pedagogical approach," says Richardson. "Information literacy should not be viewed as a technology curriculum separate from course curriculum, but more as a way to reconceive teaching and learning."

In fact, once teachers get the help they need to get started, many find that Web tools allow them to do the kinds of things they want to do in the classroom, such as promoting project-based learning, collaborative learning, and critical thinking (see "Examples of Classroom Blogs, Wikis, and Podcasts").

Fortunately, there are many resources available to help teachers experiment with Web-based projects (see "How to Get Started"). In planning her fifth graders' wiki, Herzig was assisted by the school's technology director, Shelley Paul, who claimed no real prior expertise other than reading Richardson's book. Wikis, whose name comes from the Hawaiian word *wiki-wiki* meaning "quick," involve installation on a server and are more complicated to set up than blogs, which can be created more easily on the Web through available Web sites. There are about "fifty flavors" of wiki software out there, Paul says. She did no programming, but simply downloaded free software onto her school's server. She also found short-and-sweet online instructions on how to format wiki text and create links to

EXAMPLES OF CLASSROOM BLOGS, WIKIS, AND PODCASTS

Will Richardson's Modern American Literature blog on Sue Monk Kidd's *The Secret Life of Bees* at Hunterdon Central Regional High School, Flemington, N.J.
weblogs.hcrhs.k12.nj.us/bees

Eric Langhorst's class blogs with embedded podcasts on Pat Hughes's *Guerilla Season* and Gary Blackwood's *The Year of the Hangman* at South Valley Junior High School, Liberty, Mo.
www.guerrillaseason.blogspot.com
www.theyearofthehangman.blogspot.com

Meriwether Lewis Elementary School wiki with podcasts and individual teacher "Classroom Notes" blogs, Portland, Ore.
www.lewiselementary.org

Darren Kuropatwa's high school math blogs at Daniel McIntyre Collegiate Institute, Winnipeg, Canada.
Applied Math: am40sw07.blogspot.com
Pre-Calculus: pc40sw07.blogspot.com
AP Calculus: apcalc06.blogspot.com
For teachers: adifference.blogspot.com

Bob Sprankle's "Tech Time with Mr. S" podcasts at Wells Elementary School, Wells, Maine.
weskids.com
For teachers: www.bobsprankle.com

other pages. Based on this information, Paul created a one-page cheat sheet for students, who were soon transcribing research, scanning photos, making art, and posting audio portions.

Beyond technical know-how, other hurdles to using Web tools in school often include safety and privacy concerns (see "Safety Advice"). For both blogs and wikis, many safety and security issues can be addressed through the choice of platform controlling access to the site. Most schools bar students from using full names, and many teachers vet all posts before they appear. Wikis have reversal buttons for restoring vandalized sites.

Ultimately, however, many believe that safety is not enforced so much by filters, which students can often defeat, as by education—like teaching audience awareness, how to recognize cyberbullying, and the rules of online etiquette.

TAPPING THE "WOW" FACTOR

One blogging convert, Eric Langhorst, an eighth-grade teacher at South Valley Junior High in Liberty, Mo., has revamped his curriculum to include Web tools. With his students, Langhorst built a book blog—or online journal—around Pat Hughes's novel *Guerrilla Season*, which details the atrocities committed by Missouri neighbors during the Civil War. Langhorst posted questions to draw out students' opinions on what they were reading and help students make connections to current events like the war in Iraq. Students were required to submit comments to the blog anonymously or with first names only. The book's author also participated in the blog, responding to student questions and uploading podcasts on her research, which students could listen to on their computers or iPods.

In addition to motivating students by tapping into the "wow" factor, Langhorst says, blogging gives them the chance to get more involved and spend more quality time on a project, since they can work where and when they want. "They can participate in the blog at home, in the library, etc., instead of limiting their educational experience to just a 45-minute class that takes place in one location," he says.

Another benefit of the blog project was a noticeable increase in family involvement. "The biggest change I saw was that

HOW TO GET STARTED

Many Web sites provide opportunities for setting up blogs, wikis, and other nifty Web tools for educators. Many are free. For detailed help, see Will Richardson's Web site, www.weblogg-ed.com, or David Warlick's website, www.landmark-project.com.

Blogs (Web logs) are sequentially organized communication sites for exchanging information publicly or privately (within classrooms). Used as class portals, online filing cabinets for student work, or places for public conversations, blogs can include audio, video, and photo enhancements. See www.blogger.com, edublogs.org, classwebs.net, and www.classblogmeister.com. To search for blogs by keyword, visit www.technorati.com.

Wikis are content-management systems that encourage collaboration. Unlike blogs, wikis can be edited by participants. Such editing can be open (like Wikipedia's) or closed (class only). They demand some technical skill to install and are limited as text-editing tools, although some sites (called WYSIWYG, as in: What You See Is What You Get) offer editing interfaces closer to Word. See www.pbwiki.com, or seedwiki.com.

Podcasts are basically amateur radio recordings, or audio files, created using built-in computer microphones. They are edited online and then downloaded to computers, blogs, wikis, or cell phones. See audacity.sourceforge.net or download Apple's iTunes software free www.apple.com/itunes (Apple's podcast directory includes an education link).

Moodle is a free, easy-to-learn software package for educators. Installed on school servers, it features programs for creating tests, grades, forums, wikis, and blogs, and offers teachers oversight capabilities that allow them to see all a student's postings, coursework, or site visits. See docs.moodle.org/en/About_Moodle.

some of the students shared the experience of reading the novel and using the blog with their family," Langhorst says. "In one case, a student told me that she read the novel with her dad and then they both went online to read comments from the author and leave a comment. When was the last time you heard of a father and daughter reading a novel together and asking the author questions that had immediate feedback?"

A NATURAL FORUM FOR TEENS

Berkeley (Calif.) High School history teacher Ben Sanoff uses both blogs and wikis to hold online discussions for his classes. Students also submit essays—with their names removed—for peer editing. Blogs are a natural forum for teens, "who prefer to talk to their peers," he says. "You wouldn't believe how often they check the site for responses to their posts."

On the nights he requires online discussions on particular issues, Sanoff says, the students "work hard not to embarrass themselves. They want to sound smart and coherent." Because the blog gives students more time and space to organize their thoughts, he believes it gives them better opportunities to learn and model how to build logical arguments, which is especially helpful for the weaker students.

Students using the blog also get more feedback on their writing than he can provide as an individual teacher. "I have 120 students spread between five classes and can't possibly give everyone the attention they need. So I throw up a grading rubric, have them post their essays, and then comment on each other's work," he says.

Sanoff says he's never had a problem with cyberbullying because his students know that he's monitoring the classroom site. Nor does the so-called digital divide seem to be a problem. Even students without home computers participate, he says. "They seem to manage somehow, whether at a library or with friends. I worried about this before realizing that nearly

SAFETY ADVICE

- Part of teachers' Web training must be about safety. Beyond reading the Children's Internet Protection Act (www.fcc.gov/cgb/consumerfacts/cipa.html), teachers should discuss school policies around student use of the Web.

- Remind students that they are posting as representatives of the school and that their language should reflect this. They need to remember that postings are public and may be permanent.

- Talk to students about cyberbullying and the importance of treating fellow students and other Web visitors with respect. Warn them that what they publish can be subject to disciplinary action, including lawsuits.

all kids are accessing MySpace or Facebook or e-mail or something anyway all the time."

THE NEW DIGITAL DIVIDE

Teaching students to use computers creatively and collaboratively is exactly what is needed, many experts say, to bridge what they see as a new digital divide. "The digital divide no longer defines those with or without a computer," explains Tim Magner, director of the office of educational technology at the U.S. Department of Education (DOE). "Increasingly, it has more to do with degrees of Web facility." Having access to a computer, he explains, does not mean that a person can easily navigate the glut of information now available on the Web to produce something new and useful.

"Operational facility is less an end goal than a way to get to critical thinking, innovation, and invention," he says.

Indeed, the very definition of literacy must expand to include the ability to effectively research, converse, and publish through the Web, argues David F. Warlick, a former teacher and author of *Classroom Blogging: A Teacher's Guide to the Blogosphere*. "We're spending too much time teaching students about paper," he says. Citing a study by the School of Information Management and Systems at the University of California at Berkeley, Warlick points to the five "exabytes" of new information produced in 2002—enough for 37,000 more libraries the size of the Library of Congress. Of that, only .01 percent has actually been published in print. With the right skills, Warlick says, teachers can show students how to mine this expanding lode of information to create "personal digital libraries" that are far richer and more timely than any printed book.

"How to identify the specific skill set students will need in the 21st century to be computer literate—this discussion will evolve as the technology grows and changes," the DOE's Magner says. But one thing is clear, he adds: "Students need greater sophistication in using these information and communication Web tools if they wish to engage in what is becoming an increasingly complex future."

This chapter originally appeared in the May/June 2007 issue of the Harvard Education Letter.

FOR FURTHER READING

How Much Information? 2003. Available online at http://www2.sims.berkeley.edu/research/projects/how-much-info-2003/execsum.htm

W. Richardson. *Blogs, Wikis, Podcasts, and Other Powerful Web Tools for the Classroom*. Thousand Oaks, CA: Corwin Press, 2006.

D. R. Warlick. *Classroom Blogging: A Teacher's Guide to the Blogosphere*. Raleigh, NC: The Landmark Project, 2005. Available at http://landmark-project.com

N. E. Willard. *Cyberbullying and Cyberthreats: Responding to the Challenge of Online Social Aggression, Threats, and Distress*. Champaign, IL: Research Press, 2007.

CHAPTER 9

The Classroom of Popular Culture

What video games can teach us about making students *want* to learn

James Paul Gee

Why is it that many children can't sit still long enough to finish their homework and yet will spend hours playing games on the computer? Video games are spectacularly successful at engaging young learners. It's not because they are easy. Good video games are long, complex, and difficult. They have to be; if they were dumbed down, no one would want to play. But if children couldn't figure out how to play them—and have fun doing so—game designers would soon go out of business.

To succeed, game designers incorporate principles of learning that are well supported by current research. Put simply, they recruit learning as a form of pleasure. Games like *Rise of Nations*, *Age of Mythology*, *Deus Ex*, *The Elder Scrolls III: Morrowind*, and *Tony Hawk's Underground* teach children not only how to play but how to learn, and to keep on learning.

Children have to learn long, complex, and difficult things in school, too. They need to be able to learn in deep ways: to improvise, innovate, and challenge themselves; to develop concepts, skills, and relationships that will allow them to explore new worlds; to experience learning as a source of enjoyment and as a way to explore and discover who they are. Let's look at how this kind of learning works in cutting-edge video games. We might learn something ourselves.

PRODUCERS, NOT CONSUMERS

To start with, good video games offer players strong identities. In some games, players learn to view the virtual world through the eyes of a distinctive personality, like the solitary Special Forces operative Solid Snake in the espionage action game *Metal Gear Solid*. In others, like the epic role-playing game *The Elder Scrolls III: Morrowind*, each player builds a character from the ground up and explores the game from that character's point of view. Game designers recognize that learning and identity are interrelated. Learning a new domain, whether physics or furniture making, requires students to see the world in new ways—in the ways physicists or furniture makers do.

Game designers let players be producers, not just consumers. Players codesign a game through their unique actions and decisions. Many games come with software that allows players to modify ("mod") them to produce new scenarios or whole new games. For instance, in the Tony Hawk skateboarding games, players can design their own skate parks. At another level, an open-ended game like *The Elder Scrolls III: Morrowind*, in which each character undertakes his or her own journey, ultimately becomes a different experience for each player.

Players can also customize games to fit their learning and playing styles, since well-designed games allow problems to be solved in multiple ways. For example, in the two *Deus Ex* games, many of the problems a player faces can be solved in at least three ways: using stealth, confrontation, or persuasion. Many games also offer levels of play for beginning, experienced, or advanced players, letting players choose the degree of challenge they are comfortable with. In some games, players can test their own skills. For example, the real-time strategy game *Rise of Nations* asks, "How fast can you get to the Gunpowder Age? Find out if your resource-management skills are good enough."

Features like these encourage players to take risks, explore, and try new things. If they fail, the consequences are minimal—they can start over from their last saved game. All these factors give players a real sense of agency, ownership, and control. It's their game.

A CYCLE OF MASTERY

But learning goes yet deeper in well-designed games. Research has shown that when learners are left completely free to solve a complex problem, they may hit on creative solutions. But these solutions may not necessarily help them generate good hypotheses for solving later problems, even easier ones. A simple classroom example is the case of the young child who comes to think that reading means memorizing words. This may work perfectly well—until the child is swamped by the marked increase in vocabulary in more complex books (see "Playing with Words").

In good video games problems are well ordered, so that early ones lead the player to formulate hypotheses that work well for solving later, harder problems. For example, if stealth is important in a game, the first levels will clearly show the player why confrontation is a less effective option, so as not to reinforce skills that will later undermine the player's success.

This well-ordered sequence creates an ongoing cycle of consolidation and challenge that enables players to confront an initial set of problems, and then practice solving them until they have routinized their mastery. The game then throws out a new class of problem, requiring players to come up with new solutions. This phase of mastery is consolidated through

PLAYING WITH WORDS

One of the biggest predictors of success in school is the size of a child's vocabulary. Many children struggle to master the specialized language used in math, social studies, or science. But look at this typical description of a Bulbasaur, one of the Pokémon characters, from the game's trading card:

> Bulbasaur are a combination of Grass-type and Poison-type Pokémon. Because they are Grass-type Pokémon, Bulbasaur have plant-like characteristics such as the large, leafy growth on their back. Over time, Bulbasaur will evolve into Ivysaur and Venusaur.

There are lots of low-frequency words here, and complex syntax as well. The content is also challenging: There are 150 Pokémon characters, categorized into roughly 16 types. Each has a specialized set of skills, and many can evolve into one or two other characters. Yet children as young as six master the language and rules of Pokémon, and there is no evidence that socioeconomic factors have any impact on their skill or interest in the game.

repetition, only to be challenged again. In this way, good games stay within, but at the outer edge of, the player's competence. They feel doable, but challenging. This makes them pleasantly frustrating, putting players in what psychologists call a "flow" state.

Video games operate on the principle of "performance before competence." That is, players can learn as they play, rather than having to master an entire body of knowledge before being able to put it to use. Research shows that students learn best when they learn in context—that is, when they can relate words, concepts, skills, or strategies to prior experience. In fact, many students are alienated from what they learn in school because those connections and experiences are absent. Video games are simulations of new experiences and new worlds, yet they are able to engage players with languages and ways of thinking with which they have no prior experience. Players encounter new words and techniques in the context of play, not as abstract definitions or sets of rules. This holds their interest and spurs them on to develop new skills, vocabularies, relationships, and attitudes—irrespective of factors like race and class.

One way players can increase their competence is to seek advice from other players. There are Web sites and Internet chat rooms for almost any game, where players trade tips and stories, and where questions can be posted. Experts can help novices and peers can pool information. New knowledge is available just in time—when players need it—or on demand—when players ask for it.

PREPARATION FOR A COMPLEX WORLD

Finally, good video games nurture higher-order thinking skills. They encourage players to think in terms of relationships, not isolated events or facts. In a game like *Rise of Nations*, for example, players need to think about how each step they take might affect their future actions and the actions of their opponents as they try to advance their civilizations through the ages. These kinds of games encourage players to explore their options thoroughly rather than taking the straightest and swiftest path, and to reconceive their goals from time to time—good skills in a world full of complex, high-risk systems.

Video games teach players to capitalize on "smart tools," distributed knowledge, and cross-functional teams. The virtual characters one manipulates in a game are smart tools.

They have skills and knowledge of their own, which they lend to the player. For example, the citizens in *Rise of Nations* know how to build cities, but the player needs to know where to build them. In multiplayer games like *World of WarCraft*, players form teams in which each player contributes a different set of skills. Each player must master a specialty, since a Mage plays differently than a Warrior, but the players must understand each other's specializations well enough to coordinate with one another. Thus, the knowledge needed to play the games is distributed among a set of real people and their smart tools, much as in a modern science lab or high-tech workplace.

In his bestselling book *The World Is Flat*, Thomas Friedman argues that the United States is facing a looming educational crisis. Even highly skilled jobs in radiology, computer science, or engineering are being outsourced to low-cost centers. Any job that involves standardized skills can be exported. To maintain their competitive advantage, workers in industrialized countries will need to go beyond a mastery of standardized skills to become flexible, adaptive, lifelong learners of new skills (see "The Rules of the Game"). Yet U.S. schools are focused more than ever on the "basics," measuring their success with standardized tests that assess standardized skills.

It is ironic that young people today are often exposed to more creative and challenging learning experiences in popular culture than they are in school. The principles on which video-game design is based are foundational to the kind of learning that enables children to become innovators and lifelong learners. Yet how many of today's classrooms actually incorporate these principles as thoroughly and deeply as these games do? Let's ask ourselves how we can make learning in or out of school more "game-like"—not in the sense of playing games in class, but by making the experience of learning as motivating, stimulating, collaborative, and rewarding as the experience of playing a well-designed video game.

THE RULES OF THE GAME

Challenging, fun, well-designed video games incorporate important principles of learning that are solidly supported by recent research. Why can't we base our classroom instruction on the same rules?

- Create motivation for extended learning.
- Create and honor preparation for future learning.
- Create and honor "horizontal" learning experiences—letting learners try out and consolidate their skills in different contexts at the same level, rather than hurrying them from one level to the next.
- Let learners assess their own previous knowledge and learning styles.
- Build in choices from the beginning.
- Banish the word "remedial."
- Teach skills in a simplified context so learners can see how the skills fit together and how to apply them.
- Give information in multiple modes at once (print, visual, oral).
- Provide information "just in time" and "on demand."
- Let learners customize what you are offering.
- Minimize the distinction between learning and playing.
- Use developmental (not evaluative) tests that allow learners to discover the outer edge of their competence and help them operate just inside that edge.
- Allow learners to practice their skills, and then challenge them to develop new ones. Repeat.
- Ensure that learners at every level have access to knowledge that is distributed and dispersed among people, places, sites, texts, tools, and technologies.
- Create an affinity space where learners can interact with peers and masters around a shared interest.

Adapted from Situated Language and Learning, *by James Paul Gee (New York: Routledge, 2004).*

This chapter originally appeared in the November/December 2005 issue of the Harvard Education Letter.

FOR FURTHER READING

J. C. Beck and M. Wade. *Got Game: How the Gamer Generation Is Reshaping Business Forever*. Boston, MA: Harvard Business School Press, 2005.

J. P. Gee. *What Video Games Have to Teach Us about Learning and Literacy*. New York, NY: Palgrave/Macmillian, 2003.

R. Koster. *Theory of Fun for Game Design*. Phoenix, AZ: Paraglyph, 2004.

For many other papers related to games and learning, see www.academiccolab. org/

CHAPTER 10

Money and Motivation

**New initiatives rekindle debate over the link
between rewards and student achievement**

David McKay Wilson

Kids in schools across America are bringing home big
bucks.

Middle-school students in Washington, D.C., can
bank as much as $1,500 per year for high grades, good
attendance, and exemplary behavior, including wearing their
school uniforms each day. In Chicago, ninth and tenth graders can earn up to $200 every five weeks. Flunk one class and
you lose all your earnings for that grading period, but ace your
classes all year and you can earn up to $2,000. Half is payable
at the end of the year—but to collect the other half, you have
to stay in school until graduation.

The promise of cash—or "Green for Grades," as they call
it in Chicago—is the latest twist in a decades-old debate over
how best to motivate student behavior, particularly learning.
Critics of cash-based schemes say research shows that external incentives may bring short-term results, but fail to help
students develop a curious intellect and the intrinsic desire to
learn. Once the money stream runs dry, critics say, research
indicates that students will revert to their old ways and may

even regress. Indeed, similar programs in some public schools have failed in the past.

Despite these concerns, the idea of using cash awards in public elementary, middle, and high schools appears to be gaining traction, fueled by research grants from private and corporate foundations. Arne Duncan, former CEO of the Chicago Public Schools who in January became the U.S. Secretary of Education, believes the drop-out problem is urgent enough to justify more experimentation with monetary rewards. In Chicago, Duncan says, he was "fighting for the lives" of inner-city teens, who need high school diplomas to gain a foothold in the local workforce. "If they stay in school, it shapes the rest of their lives," he says. "It's make-or-break time. We need to keep them engaged."

Duncan points out that some inner-city teens are being recruited by drug dealers who can provide jobs for those in financial straits. If it takes money to woo a student from the streets to the classroom, he says, it's worth it. Paying students also increases the allure of achievement: Students who get lots of A's now have the fattest wallets. "We are giving cash to those who are working the hardest, and they are now the stars," Duncan says.

"THE 'SAME OLD' STRATEGIES HAVE FAILED"

The incentive programs that have gained the most attention are those developed by economist Roland Fryer Jr. and his colleagues at the Education Innovation Laboratory (Ed Labs) at Harvard University. Housed within Harvard's Institute for Quantitative Social Science, the Ed Labs were established in 2008 with a $44 million grant from the Eli and Edythe Broad Foundation. The Ed Labs pilot programs offer a wide range of short-term monetary incentives to inner-city students who have not yet thrived in school (see "Pilot Programs Experiment with Cash Rewards"). Ed Labs researchers plan to collect data

PILOT PROGRAMS EXPERIMENT WITH CASH REWARDS

In 2008, the Education Innovation Laboratory at Harvard University unveiled three pilot programs testing the use of cash incentives for students:

- In Chicago, 3,700 students in 20 high schools can earn $50 for each A, $35 for each B, and $20 for each C. If a student fails a class, the student will lose all money earned for that grading period. However, the student can recoup those lost earnings by completing the credit needed to pass the class. Half the money is given to the student; the other half is distributed upon graduation.
- New York City is paying 6,000 students in 58 schools each time they take one of the district's 10 periodic assessments, given in fourth grade and seventh grade. Fourth graders receive $5 to complete each test and can earn up to $20 more, depending on their score. The incentives are doubled for seventh graders.
- In Washington, D.C., 2,700 students in 14 middle schools can earn up to $1,500 a year. Money is dispersed every two weeks, based on a rubric that measures their progress in five areas: attendance, behavior, and three academic indicators chosen by school principals. The school offers classes on financial literacy to address the issues that may arise for 12-year-olds with bountiful bank accounts at their behest.

to evaluate these and other programs with what Fryer terms "a rigorous scientific lens." He compares his experiments to randomized studies done by pharmaceutical researchers testing new drugs on sick patients. "The 'same old' strategies have failed generations of students," Fryer said upon announcement of the grant that established the Ed Labs. "There have been pockets of progress and beacons of hope, but not the systematic changes in how we educate urban youth."

In Washington, D.C., there are already signs of progress. By December 2008, attendance was up in the schools where the Ed Labs program was being piloted, and students were wearing their uniforms regularly, according to district spokeswoman Jennifer Calloway. After a year, researchers plan to compare data on attendance, behavior, and academic achievement in schools that used financial incentives with data from those that did not. "Our goals are to use short-term incentives to engage students in their own education," says Calloway. "If it doesn't work, we have no problem disbanding it."

"WE TRIED IT . . . "

Recent high-profile programs offering financial rewards for performance either have failed or were phased out in favor of new attempts, according to those familiar with them. For example, in 2006, school officials in Chelsea, Mass., offered $25 each quarter to every student with perfect attendance. Two years later, the district discontinued the program. Superintendent Thomas Kingston says the incentive didn't raise attendance at all. "We tried it and it didn't work," he says. "We rewarded those who showed up, and [it] didn't have a measurable effect on the kids who weren't coming. They weren't enticed by the incentive."

The same year, district officials in Chicago offered up to $500 for groceries or up to $1,000 for rent or mortgage payments to students with perfect attendance in the first three months of the year. That program has now been phased out, as other programs were established at individual schools so that educators could better track the impact of the incentives, according to Chicago Public Schools spokesman Frank Shuftan.

In 2007, New York City officials provided students in seven high schools with cell phones and granted free minutes based on performance. The project ran over a four-month period—long enough to demonstrate the technical viability of the model, but not to determine if it was actually effective.

Gavin Samms, research director at Harvard's Ed Labs, acknowledges that researchers aren't yet sure what kinds of rewards work in school settings. In addition to testing programs that reward outcomes, such as the Ed Labs' pilot programs in New York, Washington, and Chicago, he says, he and his colleagues plan to test incentives on what he calls "inputs," such as the effort necessary to read a book or complete homework. "We want to see if this is the right set of models," he says. "If not, then we know they don't work, and that's helpful too."

"GOING FOR THE QUICK FIX"

Researchers like Edward Deci, Gowan Professor of Social Sciences at the University of Rochester, say policymakers who favor the use of financial incentives are ignoring decades of research on motivation. "They are all going for the quick fix," Deci says. "It might work over the short term, but the longer-term consequences are all negative."

In a 1999 paper, Deci reviewed 128 scientific studies and concluded that tangible rewards had a negative effect on intrinsic motivation and actually decreased motivation for interesting activities, with students reverting to their earlier behavior once the reward is terminated. "It couldn't be clearer," he says. "It's sexy to pay kids. It seems cool. And it's easier to pay them than to ask the real critical question—what do these schools have to do to facilitate self-motivation?"

Sara Wilford, director of Sarah Lawrence College's Art of Teaching program and a member of its psychology faculty, calls the cash incentives "behavior modification in the most crass way." "It may be a sweetener to get them in, but what is going to keep them?" Wilford asks. "Pay them more money?"

Other research, however, indicates that the effect of tangible rewards like cash may depend on a student's level of interest. In a review of 145 studies, Judy Cameron, professor of educational psychology at the University of Alberta, concluded that in cases where subjects have low interest in a task, tangible rewards could increase motivation and performance. Moreover, she did not find negative effects for rewarding high-interest tasks—as long as the rewards were given after the task was completed.

CULTIVATING A "GROWTH MIND-SET"

An alternative to cash incentives is the effort to cultivate student attitudes that support high achievement. Carol Dweck, Lewis and Virginia Eaton Professor of Psychology at Stanford University, says her research shows that students with a "growth mind-set"—the belief that the ability to learn can be cultivated and improved through hard work—develop the kind of inner motivation that spurs strong performance. Students with a "fixed mind-set," who see intelligence as a finite entity to be tapped, tended to give up when faced with tough challenges, Dweck found. She suggests that instead of offering external rewards, schools should help students develop a growth mind-set (see "Motivating Achievement in Algebra").

During five years in the late 1990s, Dweck followed four waves of middle-school students through seventh and eighth grades. The students in each cohort were divided into an experimental group and a control group. During several workshop sessions, Dweck's team taught students in the experimental group that the brain's neurons make new connections when they learn, that the brain is like a muscle that gets stronger with use, and that students could "grow" their intelligence by studying. Both the experimental group and the control group

MOTIVATING ACHIEVEMENT IN ALGEBRA

Educators in four school districts are piloting a program to improve ninth graders' performance in algebra, based on Stanford psychologist Carol Dweck's research on motivation and University of Texas mathematician Uri Treisman's work with peer groups. Treisman's Emerging Scholars program, now replicated in about 200 college and universities, develops peer groups that provide support for first-year college students taking calculus.

"Often a peer can explain a problem in a way that's different from the instructor," says Gloria White, managing director of the Charles A. Dana Center at the University of Texas at Austin, which is collecting data on the project. "We think it will be effective for ninth graders."

The Academic Youth Development project, carried out in Arlington, Va.; Evanston, Ill.; Madison, Wis.; and Shaker Heights, Ohio, brings together teachers and up to 30 students for a two- or three-week summer session before the students enter ninth grade. In addition to algebra readiness—concepts such as proportionality and problem solving—the students are taught that through effort and persistence, they can build their brains to improve their math skills.

"We call it effective effort," says Laura Cooper, assistant superintendent for curriculum and instruction in Evanston.

The students also become part of collaborative learning communities, in which they become comfortable working in teams and sharing strategies to attack thorny math problems.

"Our early results are promising," Cooper notes. "Our 14-year-olds, who have failed in the past and thought their academic careers were over, have realized that they can learn, and that 14 isn't too late to start learning."

were taught mnemonic devices to augment their study skills. Dweck found that the students in the experimental group became much more engaged in learning, set higher goals for themselves, and responded to academic challenges with more effort. Those students maintained that approach over two years. "We tell the students to imagine your brain and realize that you form new connections when you work on something hard and learn something new," says Dweck. "Not only does it help—it's true. It unlocks intrinsic motivation, and the kids get smarter."

A computer-based version of Dweck's approach, which was tested in 20 New York City schools in 2003, showed a sharp rise in participating students' grades and motivation to learn. "Virtually every student in the New York City study said the workshop changed the way they studied and the way they paid attention in class," says Dweck. She's now testing the computer-based program with 1,000 home-schooled students and hopes to disseminate it once the results from her latest study are complete.

This chapter originally appeared in the March/April 2009 issue of the Harvard Education Letter.

FOR FURTHER READING

L. S. Blackwell, K. H. Trzesniewski, and C. S. Dweck. "Implicit Theories of Intelligence Predict Achievement Across an Adolescent Transition: A Longitudinal Study and an Intervention." *Child Development* 78 (January 2007): 246–263.

J. Cameron. "Negative Effects of Reward on Intrinsic Motivation—A Limited Phenomenon: Comment on Deci, Koestner, and Ryan." *Review of Educational Research* 71 (Spring 2001): 29.

The Charles A. Dana Center, www.utdanacenter.org/academicyouth/index.php

Edward Deci. Self-Determination Theory, www.psych.rochester.edu/SDT/

The Education Innovation Laboratory at Harvard University, www.edlabs. harvard.edu

C. Mueller and C. Dweck. "Praise for Intelligence Can Undermine Children's Motivation and Performance." *Journal of Personality & Social Psychology* 75 (July 1998): 33–53.

CHAPTER 11

"Manga Is My Life"

Opportunities (and opportunities missed) for literacy development

Michael Bitz

As the founder of the Comic Book Project—a literacy initiative for underserved youths—I am often asked if I read comic books as a child. Because the answer is no, I am consistently amazed by children who discover comic books as literature—and equally dismayed by educators who ban such books, chosen by children, from the classroom.

The idea behind the Comic Book Project is simple: children plan, write, design, and produce original comic books, then publish and distribute their work for other children to use as learning and motivational tools. Since its inception in 2001, the project has grown to encompass over 50,000 youths across the country, mostly in high-poverty urban schools and neighborhoods. More than just a fun and motivational project for children, the project is intended to model how creative thinking can bolster academic success. The thousands of comics created by youth participants in the Comic Book Project are a testament to the power of the medium for building conventional literacy skills, including spelling, grammar, punctuation, sentence structure, character development, narrative flow, editing, revising, presenting, and publishing—all of the skills that we aim to instill in young readers and writers.

I saw this firsthand in observing a group of students in the afterschool comic book club at Martin Luther King Jr. High School in Manhattan over a period of several years. During school, many of these students—African American and Latino teenagers—struggled academically and socially. But after school, when the grade books were closed and the textbooks tossed back into lockers, these same students—so disengaged from the life of the classroom—became highly motivated readers and writers.

WHIMSICAL HEROES

If you imagine these students inventing new versions of Superman, Wonder Woman, or any other popular American superhero, prepare for a surprise. The adolescents who convened every Thursday afternoon to create comics were fully entrenched in *manga*: Japanese comic books. They consumed volume after volume of their favorite series such as *Bleach* and *D.Gray-Man*, which were originally published in Japanese and then translated into English.

The students' own comic book creations reflected their devotion to manga—characters with saucer-shaped eyes and flowing hair, storylines with whimsical twists and turns, and an aesthetic focused on the whimsical rather than super-powerful. Many of the students gave themselves Japanese nicknames and began to teach themselves some Japanese words and phrases. Some imagined themselves visiting Tokyo, interspersed among thousands of people at a *doujinshi* convention for amateur comic book creators just like them. One student's statement captured the group's collective commitment to this uniquely Japanese art and literature: "Manga is my life."

The club's meetings on Thursday afternoons became a haven of creative and social development for the participating

TIME AGO THERE WAS A FOX DEMON GIRL NAMED CASANDRA. SHE WAS BORN HALF FOX AND HALF HUMAN. SHE THINKS HER LIFE WOULD BE HAPPIER IF SHE WAS ALL HUMAN, SO HERE IS HER STORY.

teenagers. They eagerly opened their sketchbooks and drafted Japanese-inspired designs, while developing and sharing story lines related to their personal and cultural identities.

The weekly club meetings were also a sturdy buttress for literacy development. In planning and designing their comics, the students amassed an extraordinary amount of writing. They explored narrative elements of tone and atmosphere with their word choices. They delved into the complexities of punctuation and sentence structure in considering the voice of a character and how the reader would perceive the text. They shared their work with each other, establishing a peer-review process in order to get their manga ready for the annual school publication. The comics went through several revisions, each leading to higher-quality writing and artistic design. When the comics were complete, many of the works were on par with the professional manga with which the students were so enamored. And in publishing and distributing their original manga, these students gained recognition as writers and artists in New York City and beyond. They were inducted, as literacy expert Lucy Calkins says, as insiders into the world of authorship.

The high school participants in this club acted as a cohort— a collective of like-minded artists and writers wholeheartedly dedicated to the craft of manga. Yet they were also individuals, each with a unique style and approach, and each with a different set of life circumstances outside the club room. Samantha, for example, used her sketchbook as a personal diary, transforming her everyday experiences into manga stories.

One of those stories features Samantha at an anime convention where she falls in love with a boy in "cosplay"—short for "costume play" or dress-up. The boy turns out to be a girl; the comical story ends with Samantha, shamelessly crushed, saying: "So . . . I've learned that *bishounen* at anime cons may, in fact, not even be a *shounen* . . . " Translation: an attractive male teenager at an anime convention may not even be an immature young boy.

Another student, Reggie, designed a comic book featuring African American samurai warriors. In contrast to the random violence that marked Reggie's life, his characters systematized violent confrontations through scheduled battles. Following the code of the samurai, they fought for justice and respect with a combination of personal convictions and sharp swords.

While Reggie was prolific, Treasure struggled to create manga, unsure of her abilities. Over time, and with the support of other club members, however, Treasure produced some of the club's most impressive comics. Her growth as a comic book creator led to a scholarship for a weeklong workshop this summer at the Center for Cartoon Studies in Vermont.

And Keith, a boy who struggled with abuse and homelessness, developed a comic book character named the Hunter, who, in Keith's words, represented "my dark persona, or at least how my persona would've been if I decided to go about solving my problems the angry and negative way."

Of course, these adolescents did not succeed at creating and publishing manga on their own. A number of key adults at the afterschool program supported their efforts (see "Anatomy of a Comic Book Club"). The program director, staff, and volunteers encouraged the academic and artistic growth of the students, but they also became surrogate guardians, social workers, and guidance counselors when other adults in the students' lives were absent.

ANATOMY OF A COMIC BOOK CLUB

There is no right or wrong way to go about forming a comic book club, and different populations of learners require different approaches. For example, the club at Martin Luther King Jr. High School did not start out with a focus on manga, but the participants' interests propelled the club in that direction. Below are some suggestions for launching and sustaining a club.

- **Designating an instructor.** Ideal club instructors are educators with the ability to motivate and inspire. These educators do not need to be artists or art educators. In some cases, the abilities of an experienced artist may establish an unbridgeable gulf between educator and learner. The instructor should also be an accommodating problem solver and someone who is sensitive to the issues in a child's life.
- **Recruiting students.** Administrators can recruit participants by posting flyers and making announcements, but they may want to approach individual students—for instance, those who exhibit artistic abilities or who get into trouble for drawing when they should be doing something else. Other potential students may be those who lack direction and would benefit from participating in a structured activity.
- **Finding a space.** The club should meet in a well-lit room with large tables around which students can arrange their chairs to work together. Although some afterschool programs are housed in the cafeteria, consider factors such as the quality of light, noise level, access to clean work surfaces, and whether seats and tables can be easily rearranged to foster collaboration.

(continued)

- **Scheduling.** While the club may meet only once a week, members should be expected to reflect and practice between sessions—reading comics and researching new styles; practicing drawing, writing, and inking; and consulting with other members.
- **Materials and supplies.** Besides blank typing paper, pencils, and a variety of black pens, the club should provide a light box for tracing drawings onto quality paper; a flatbed scanner; and a computer equipped with Adobe Photoshop, which students can use to add color to their drawings.
- **Publishing and exhibiting.** Publishing their work in print and online drives students to complete their comics—a difficult mission for those who are perfectionists or who struggle to manage their time. Seeing their names and work in print, creating exhibits, and presenting their work to the public reaffirm for students the quality of their work and their ability to inspire others.

The most influential adult for the teenagers was the club instructor, Phil DeJean. An art teacher during school hours, Phil was a comic book fanatic. His broad range of knowledge of everything comics—including manga—helped him connect to the youths who felt so isolated from their teachers and peers at school. Phil helped the students move from replications of popular cartoon characters to well-crafted original manga, full of intricate details of language and design. He differentiated his instruction to meet the needs of every student—some needed more support with their writing skills, others with the drawing of hands and feet, still others with the self-confidence necessary for creating something unique, independent, and original. The students held Phil in high regard, and their commitment to the comic book club—and, in turn, reading and writing—reached new heights as the students strove to produce manga at the highest possible level.

WHY ONLY IN AFTERSCHOOL?

It is not a coincidence that the comic book club at Martin Luther King Jr. High School was an afterschool program. School-based programs like this, managed by nonprofit organizations, are finding new ways to connect with youth through media, technology, and the arts. These activities are not merely fun and engaging; they are authentic pathways to literacy and learning. The participants in this particular club read an enormous number of books and created an equally voluminous collection of original writing. Moreover, their works published in print and online inspired scores of other students all across the United States and around the world. A young girl from Florida, for example, downloaded one of the school publications from the Comic Book Project Web site and then sent the following e-mail:

> Thank you for the amazing manga! I have some questions for the autors [*sic*]: Is the fox-girl character always both forms or does sometimes she just act like a girl and then become the fox. How did she get her powers? Was it magic or was she born with them? Do her powers ever get her into trouble? How did her little cat get her powers? Why do they eat so much soup? Do you have any advice for me on how to draw manga like you did? Can you PLEASE send me a copy with autograph of the artists!

It is a shame that there weren't more opportunities for the comic book club members, so excited about words and language, to pursue their passions in English, social studies, and other school classes. It is unfortunate that they had to wait for one afternoon each week to explore and celebrate the world of authorship. There could have been countless opportunities for students to connect a whimsical fairy from, say, the popular manga *Oh My Goddess!* to Ariel in *The Tempest*. They could have explored manga as a construct of Japanese culture and its evolution from World War II to today. The learning opportunities are infinite, bound only by the creativity of students and the willingness of an educator to think with an open mind.

This particular club opened my eyes to an important lesson: In our pursuit of basic skill reinforcement and heightened academic performance, we educators ought to look at the opportunities right in front of us before we lose another generation of students ready and eager to learn. If this means putting aside the textbook for a Japanese-style comic book, why not take that leap?

This chapter originally appeared in the July/August 2009 issue of the Harvard Education Letter. *It is adapted from* Manga High: Literacy, Identity, and Coming of Age in an Urban High School *(Harvard Education Press).*

FOR FURTHER READING

The Comic Book Project, www.comicbookproject.org

Center for Cartoon Studies, www.cartoonstudies.org

National Association of Comics Art Educators, www.teachingcomics.org

Shojo Manga Project, www.csuchico.edu/~mtoku/vc/Exhibitions/girlsmangaka/girlsmangaka_index.html

PART III

Reaching Beyond the Classroom

CHAPTER 12

The "Quiet" Troubles of Low-Income Children

Richard Weissbourd

When many Americans think of at-risk, low-income kids, we may imagine young children who are disruptive and aggressive, ricocheting around the classroom. Or we may picture teenagers caught up with drugs or gangs, pregnant girls, or homes where parents are absent or abusive.

These images are powerful, but they badly distort who at-risk children are and what makes them vulnerable. Most of the troubles poor at-risk children have are not "loud" problems like disruptive behavior or gang involvement. They are "quiet."

I began to better understand the true nature of poor children's vulnerabilities soon after receiving my doctorate in education. I was working for the Annie E. Casey Foundation on a dropout prevention project, and I was assigned to write portraits of teenagers at risk of dropping out in Little Rock, Ark.

The first child I spoke with was staying home to take care of his mother, who was wiped out by a crushing depression. The second child I met—a lovely, shy eighth grader whose teacher described her as only thinly connected to school—was drifting along the edge of the playground, seemingly untethered to any other child. She soon revealed that this was her fifth school in two years. I met other children who were drifting out of school because they had fallen far behind or were struggling with undiagnosed learning disabilities.

But I remember thinking, "Where's my at-risk child?" None of these children matched the portrait I thought I had been assigned to write.

And then I met Randall, a handsome, stout, highly guarded seventh grader. He was involved with gangs and drugs. His teacher referred to him as a "jerk," and the principal described him as "that little asshole." I asked Randall whom he trusted and he slowly held up a piece of paper that was totally blank. Relief washed over me—I could now write my portrait! I had found my at-risk kid.

It soon dawned on me, however, that for every child I met with loud problems like Randall, I had met two or three students with quiet troubles who were also at risk. (And it's important to add that, contrary to stereotypes, I also met many well-grounded children who were making solid progress in school.)

In the years since, I have spent a great deal of time in schools working on reform efforts and as a researcher, and I have come to understand more about these quiet problems— health, emotional, academic, and social problems that are not easily discernible—and how they can undercut a student's academic prospects.

ONE PAIR OF SHOES

What exactly are these quiet problems? Why are they so often undetected? What might we do about them?

The range of these problems is vast. Hunger, dehydration, asthma, obesity, and hearing problems can all insidiously trip children up in school. Some quiet problems are psychological—depression, anxiety, the fear of utter destitution. Others are less easily categorized: not having a quiet place to read, not having money for books or a computer, not being able to manage transportation to afterschool activities. In one school outside Boston, a teacher told me that two brothers were coming to school on alternate days because they had only one pair of shoes between them.

Certain quiet problems are especially pervasive and concerning. One is *caretaking responsibility*, such as having to take care of a depressed or sick parent or look after younger siblings. One study of high school students in three cities conducted by the Institute for Survey Research at Temple University found that 20 percent of the children had missed school to take care of a "family member or close friend." Another study by the National Center for Education Statistics indicated that 12 percent of high school dropouts nationwide left school to take care of a family member. While both of these studies date back to the early 1990s, nothing in my experience indicates that circumstances have changed.

Frequent mobility also makes it hard for many children to get traction in school. It's not uncommon in urban schools for about 20 percent of the student body to change schools in a given year. A U.S. Government Accountability Office report revealed that "one-sixth of the nation's third graders—more than half a million children—have attended at least three different schools since starting first grade." In areas of highly concentrated poverty, that number is often far higher. As a result, students may bounce between schools that have entirely different curricula and teaching practices, putting them at risk of school difficulties and reducing the chance that they will stay in school.

The number of children with *undetected or untreated vision problems* is a national scandal. In any urban classroom, it's not uncommon to find one or two children squinting at their books or at the blackboard. By one estimate, at least 25 percent of urban students have uncorrected vision problems. Part of the problem is that kids lose their glasses easily, and it can take Medicaid up to six months to replace them. When the glasses do come, they're often big and clunky—the kind of glasses that no school-age child wants to wear.

Finally, *sleep deprivation* interferes with the learning of large numbers of children (see appendix, "Waking Up to Sleep Deprivation"). Staff members in one elementary school I have worked with estimate that about one-quarter of their students experience sleep deprivation consistently enough to interfere with learning. That percentage is likely to be far higher in high school.

THE "STEADY DRIZZLE" OF PARENTAL HOPELESSNESS

Just as concerning as the quiet problems that confront children are those that hinder their parents. While many quiet problems can afflict parents, parental depression is especially concerning. Somewhere between 10 percent and 20 percent of parents will suffer from acute, severe depression, experiencing some combination of fatigue, loss of appetite, withdrawal, hopeless moods, and suicidal thoughts. But a range of studies suggests that 30 percent to 60 percent of low-income parents will suffer from more moderate depression for longer periods of time. I am not talking about mental illness. I am talking about the steady drizzle of helplessness and hopelessness that can afflict those trapped in poverty for many years, especially when these adults are isolated and in constant stress.

Many of these people, despite their depression, are warm, effective parents—a feat that requires no small amount of pluck and courage. But children of depressed parents are more likely to suffer from an array of problems, including developmental delays, juvenile delinquency, and depression. What's more, it's far harder for depressed parents to do the things critical for their children's school success. The strongest predictor of school success for a young child is growing up in a language-rich environment, a place where parents are not only reading but asking questions, listening, and engaging in rich, ongoing conversation. All of these activities can be exhausting for a depressed parent.

Some schools are dealing effectively with some of these quiet problems. For example, there are districts and schools that use social workers to help families deal with housing problems—a prime reason families move—so their kids can stay in one school. Other districts are vigilant about conducting vision screenings and supplying students with eyeglasses. And I know of at least one school that arranges mental health services for depressed parents.

But these problems often slip under the radar of school staff. A study I conducted along with Harvard Graduate School of Education faculty member Terrence Tivnan, former faculty member Caroline Watts, and several graduate students indicated that some teachers fail to detect vision and hearing problems and sleep deprivation. Kids who are depressed and withdrawn can also escape teachers' notice. One reason may be that teachers are often consumed by small numbers of students with loud problems. Teachers may also stop registering these quieter problems because they know that their schools don't have the resources or time to deal with them.

As one school counselor puts it, "You have to be extraordinarily withdrawn to be referred to me."

A DATA-DRIVEN APPROACH

There are many strategies to help stem these quiet troubles. Some will require schools to partner with other agencies. For example, it's clear that schools should not be expected to take on a problem like parental depression by themselves. They could, however, ally with public health departments, community health centers, and other community agencies to reduce parental isolation and to provide the kind of public education that will help parents obtain treatment. Schools might indicate through newsletters and posters on walls, for example, the signs of parental depression and provide information about obtaining treatment. Schools can also work with community health centers to prevent sleep deprivation among children—for example, by coordinating messages to parents about the importance of establishing bedtime routines and reducing late-night television watching.

To address quiet problems effectively, it's also critical for schools to develop data-driven implementation and accountability systems. While there's a great deal of talk these days about data-driven instruction, schools are rarely driven by any data in their efforts to address other dimensions of school life. In response to a problem like sleep deprivation, say, schools will typically conduct a workshop that might be attended by a dozen parents. That's quite different from tracking the number of children who are coming to school sleep deprived, devising an intervention that seeks to engage a wide array of parents, monitoring whether it had any impact, and revising it if necessary.

The effectiveness of schools' efforts will depend on one other factor: meaningful, deep, respectful parental engagement. To deal with many of these problems, school staff will need to work closely with parents, especially the parents of those children most at risk.

Dealing with these problems will be no simple matter for school staff strapped for time and resources. Further, it's vital that efforts to deal with these problems don't drain attention away from the critical work of improving instruction. Better instruction is not only central to improving achievement: Children are far better able to manage these quiet problems when they're in classrooms where teaching is rich and engaging.

But a fairly small amount of effort in dealing with these quiet problems can go a long way toward preventing serious problems—and cutting costs. Getting kids the right eyeglasses may help prevent reading failure, for example, and reading failure is a prime reason that children end up in special education, at considerable expense. Helping a family arrange babysitting—something a parent liaison or school social worker might do—may enable a teenager to stay in school. And while mental health services for children suffering from anxiety and depression are expensive, it's hard to imagine how any society with a modicum of humanity can let these problems go untreated.

We need to make these problems visible and make them a priority in our school policies.

This chapter originally appeared in the March/April 2008 issue of the Harvard Education Letter.

CHAPTER 11 APPENDIX:
WAKING UP TO STUDENT SLEEP DEPRIVATION
Sue Costello and Richard Weissbourd

In 2007, school staff at the Lee Academy Pilot School, a public school for children age three through third grade in Dorchester, Mass., became concerned about the number of children across grades who were regularly coming to school too tired to focus and stay engaged. Instead of hosting a parent workshop on sleep deprivation, which might be attended by only a few parents, the school social worker and a social work intern decided to conduct an action-research project to gather data on the problem and discern the causes of sleep deprivation among students.

(continued)

The social workers began by asking parents of children in one preschool classroom to track evening activities in their households from 7 p.m. until wake-up the next morning. They sent a letter home informing families that they were trying to better understand the connection between sleep routines and classroom behavior and that they would be contacting the parents by phone for a brief, 10-minute conversation about their child's sleep habits and bedtime routine. Parents were also asked to fill out a chart showing how much time the child spent reading, watching TV, or playing video games in the evening; when the child went to bed; with whom the child slept; and whether the child woke up independently or had to be awakened. In addition, parents had the opportunity to participate in a follow-up phone conversation, for which they received a thank-you "sleepy time" gift. About 60 percent of the parents participated. The study found that children were getting an average of 9.5 hours of sleep at night, well below the 11.5–12 hours that three- and four-year-olds need.

Simultaneously, the classroom teacher observed and tracked the behaviors, mood, and academic engagement of each student. She saw a connection between the amount of sleep children had and their behavior and mood. The children getting less sleep and who were sleepy when they were awakened in the morning tended to be more irritable, teary, and distracted and had more difficulty controlling impulses.

The social workers then conducted face-to-face interviews with five of the participating families and phone interviews with several others to solicit additional information about what their evenings were like—for example, did they eat meals together? How often did the child have caffeine during the day? How many evenings during the week did the caretaker and child read together? Was there a consistent routine to help the child wind down? They also asked about who the child was sleeping with, the number of people living in the home, the level of financial stress, the work hours for adults in the home, and any family history of mental illness.

The data they gathered revealed many reasons that children weren't getting enough sleep. A common problem was television use. Some three- and four-year-old children were watching television until nine or ten at night and then sleeping with the television on. Another common problem was finding a comfortable, quiet place to sleep. Children's sleep was frequently compromised because they were sleeping on poor mattresses or sharing mattresses with relatives. Many families had other adult family members living with them for cultural and financial reasons, which sometimes created overcrowding and noise that made sleep difficult.

Sleep troubles can have many other causes, including hunger, poor nutrition, and anxiety, as well as various medical conditions. The follow-up interviews indicated that some parents were too stressed and overwhelmed to establish regular bedtime routines, often because they were working in the evening. One 24-year-old single mother of three children ages 10, 3, and 2 spoke poignantly about how her untreated depression interfered with her ability to be engaged in her family's evening routine. Most evenings, she said, "I want to lie down and I have to remind myself that my kids need me to help out. My 10-year-old son tells me, 'Mommy, I know you're tired, but we still need to eat.' He helps out a lot."

Rather than jumping in to try to solve these sleep-related problems, the social workers asked parents the general question: "Since sleep deprivation is a problem for many kids at

(continued)

our school, what do you think would help students sleep better?" The parents were very open to strategizing ways to get their children to sleep earlier and had a host of ideas for helping other parents at the school. Although television habits had emerged as an important issue, some parents said that television had become an ingrained aspect of bedtime routines and that it would be hard to simply turn off the television. Instead, they had other suggestions, including a school mattress drive. In addition, all parents—regardless of their own reading level or interest—spoke proudly of their children's excitement about and love of reading, which school staff realized could be an avenue for introducing new bedtime routines.

This year, staff members at the Lee Academy intend to follow up on the results of this study by providing education and concrete help on this issue to parents throughout the school. For instance, the school is implementing a schoolwide home reading campaign that will have many positive benefits, including helping families incorporate more reading—and less television—into the evening bedtime routines. Other plans include posting ongoing articles in the weekly newsletter on bedtime tips and strategies and establishing a parent resource-exchange board to help families who need beds find them. School staff members also plan to track the number of children coming to school sleep deprived to monitor the effectiveness of these interventions, so that these strategies can be adjusted and new strategies developed as need be.

CHAPTER 13

Beyond the Discipline Handbook

An interview with George Sugai

Over the past 25 years, Gallup polls have consistently reported that disruptive behavior and discipline problems in school are some of the top concerns of school staff and community members. In fact, problems with classroom management are among the most common reasons that teachers leave their jobs.

In response, many schools are turning to more formal approaches to school discipline and classroom management. One such approach is called Schoolwide Positive Behavioral Supports (PBS). About 7,500 schools across 40 states are now implementing variations of Schoolwide PBS. George Sugai, a professor of special education in the Neag School of Education at the University of Connecticut and codirector of the Center on Positive Behavioral Interventions and Supports, spoke to HEL *contributor Mitch Bogen about how PBS differs from traditional school discipline.*

What is Schoolwide Positive Behavioral Supports (PBS)?

Schoolwide PBS is a three-tiered framework for implementing schoolwide practices and systems aimed at preventing behavioral problems. In the first tier, all students should be exposed to a formal, positive, preventive, social-skills curriculum that supports the academic mission of the school. And they should be exposed to it across all settings in the school, including places outside the classroom, like in the cafeteria and on the bus. If a school does a good job with school-wide social skills, they'll support about 70 to 80 percent of the students, which means that those students should be doing pretty well from a disciplinary or behavioral perspective.

That also means about 20 percent to 30 percent of the students are still going to need more than the general curriculum. These students have trouble responding appropriately to classroom and schoolwide behavioral norms. They repeatedly break the rules, need to be reminded over and over again raise their hands or to stay in line, have difficulty following directions or participating appropriately in class, and so forth. These students should receive interventions in the top two tiers of the approach.

At the second tier, students receive extra, more intensified help, often in small groups. This could include targeted social-skills instruction, cognitive-behavioral counseling, and conflict management.

At the third tier, we typically see high levels of adult contact and monitoring. That could mean meeting one on one with a counselor or a special ed person; having adults provide frequent positive reinforcement, reminders, and prompts around desired behavior; or bringing in a mental health specialist who meets with the student, the family, and the school staff about the best ways to respond to the student's needs. The key is that it's individualized.

How do students move through the tiers?

We always avoid labeling students. Instead of saying, "He's a second-tier student" or "She's a third-tier student," it's more appropriate to label what the student does, for example, "This student needs tier two supports because of noncompliant behavior." We should be identifying what the student's challenges are *and* what he or she is doing well, because students have profiles that actually require different levels and intensities of intervention. For example, a student might do very well with most first-tier interventions but may have specific issues—difficulty following teacher directives, or responding aggressively to teasing, for example—that require third-tier supports.

In fact, behaviors such as conflict management, bullying prevention, teaching respect, or cooperative learning are taught across all three tiers. What distinguishes the tiers is the size of the grouping, the frequency of interaction, and the level of adult supervision.

In your view, what do most schools get wrong when it comes to discipline?

Most schools that I've encountered have a formal commitment to being positive, preventive, and proactive, which is the goal of Schoolwide PBS. The problem is that, in actual practice, too much time is spent reacting to negative behaviors, which is a natural tendency, and positive behavior isn't actually taught. What we see instead are high levels of office referrals, with a lot of administrator time devoted to a small number of students. You hear a steady stream of verbal reprimands and corrections: "Stop that!" "You're not following my directions!" "Why aren't you listening to me!" What happens is the intensity of these reprimands tends to increase, often in the direction of removing the student. Why removal? Because it gets rid of the "problem."

Usually, schools and classrooms ask for the kind of help that PBS offers when removal proves ineffective. "We've suspended him 12 times and there's no change," they say.

What should these schools do differently?

For the students who repeatedly display problem behavior, the approach should *not* be to make the code of conduct stricter. The code of conduct is for students who have learned the rules and expectations and are basically doing OK socially. It inhibits problem behavior and signals to a student that he or she has made a mistake. We argue that the code of conduct is really a screening tool for knowing which students need more than what is typically available.

Think of a student who is academically and socially competent. The high school discipline system is designed for her: It provides boundaries for what's OK and not OK and inhibits rule-violating behavior. If she does try sneaking a smoke in the bathroom and gets caught, in-school detention and a call home are likely to work.

But for the student who chronically smokes in the bathroom, is noncompliant, and has trouble getting along with adults, schools make the mistake of "getting tougher" and giving warnings: "One more time and you're gone!" The assumption is that if you get tougher, at some point the student will give in. But these students are already good at noncompliance and being highly resistant to our threats. In fact, what we think is a punishment is actually reinforcement for these students. Being sent to the office is actually a way to get more peer and adult attention or get out of a class; suspension gives them "permission" to go home to be with friends, watch TV, or play computer games. These students need tier two or three supports, not more tier one.

What's your position on zero-tolerance policies that remove students from school?

We're not proponents of zero-tolerance policies. But we do acknowledge that there have to be strategies for maintaining safety. Sometimes a student does need to be removed. Sometimes a metal detector or a camera or a security guard or school resource officer may be necessary for safety. But these interventions don't actually teach students the right way to behave or strengthen appropriate social skills. The literature shows that if we only employ these safety tactics, student behavior doesn't improve much.

How is PBS implemented in a school?

We begin by setting up a leadership team with the capacity to implement Schoolwide PBS. The team includes an administrator, a family member, grade-level representatives, specialists, and nonclassroom staff, such as bus drivers and cafeteria workers. It's important to include people from nonclassroom settings, because half the problem behaviors occur outside the classroom context.

The school has to create a common purpose statement by teaching and encouraging a small number of values, social skills, and expectations to everyone—things like respect, responsibility, and safety; or cooperation and problem solving.

Teaching these positive behaviors should be taken seriously, like the way we teach reading, math, or music. If you are going to teach respect, students need to know what respect looks like everywhere, in the classroom or the cafeteria or the hallway or on the bus. At the elementary level, they often teach these expectations through role playing; for the middle school, it's practice; at the high school level, it's discussion.

Students also need to receive feedback on their behavior, including recognition, acknowledgment, and positive reinforcement. Bus drivers can give out "bus bucks" for positive behavior; teachers can give special privileges to a class that's meeting its social-skills goals. Some schools even use "positive office referrals," where teachers "write students up" when they catch them doing something well. It's all about creating ceremonies and events that shift the environment from focusing on negatives to focusing on positives.

Next, a continuum of consequences for rule violations must be put in place, often in the form of the discipline handbook or code of conduct. Finally, the school has to be committed to monitoring the impact of its interventions. One of the easiest and most useful things to do is to look at discipline referral rates. Do citations for the number of classroom-managed and office-managed problem behaviors decrease? Schools also can look for an increase in those positive citations I just mentioned. A third thing to do is gather survey data to find out if the climate has become more positive as perceived by students, staff, and family members.

What kind of improvements do schools see once they have implemented this approach?

There are now three randomized-control trial studies about Schoolwide PBS implementation. They show a decrease in disciplinary actions inside the school. They show an increase in the perceived behavioral health of the school and in academic engagement. Schools also tell us that PBS is actually doable and can be implemented accurately. We also have trends showing improvement in state achievement scores for elementary students. For example, schools that have PBS in place tend to have higher scores on their early literacy state assessments, but we haven't shown that this relationship is causal.

Does Schoolwide PBS work equally well at the middle and high school levels?

I'm confident about what we've learned about elementary and middle schools' implementation, but with high schools, I don't think we've yet learned as much. We have some sites that do a pretty good job, but we haven't documented their success through experimental studies like we have with elementary and middle schools. One issue is that the high school culture may not support this kind of approach. In high schools, letting students fail is often seen as acceptable. If a student is flunking AP physics, we are less likely to reteach than to transfer the student to a less challenging class. Similarly, it's not uncommon to hear a teacher say to a student who is misbehaving, "If you don't want to be here, fine. You can leave!" Although school staff may have identified the need for PBS, some staff members don't accept the notion that a different, preventive approach should be taken with students who chronically break the rules. Instead, compliance is expected and enforced.

How can schools integrate PBS into all the other initiatives they may be undertaking?

Schools are often mandated to implement a variety of programs, such as character ed, antidrug efforts, bully proofing, and dropout prevention programs, rather than focusing on strategies and interventions tailored to their specific needs. We recently worked with a middle school on just this issue. When they looked at their discipline data, they found that the vast majority of their referrals were for a small number of behaviors, such as tardiness, noncompliance with rules in common areas, and aggressive behavior. So for the first month of school, they selected lessons from their preexisting, social-skills program that were most relevant to those specific problem behaviors. They didn't just march through the program in the order suggested by that curriculum.

PBS is really about getting districts and schools to use their minutes more wisely and to organize and implement carefully selected interventions along the three-tier continuum. PBS schools have many more positive than negative student-teacher interactions, visitors find these schools more welcoming and safe, and teaching and learning are maximized.

This chapter originally appeared in the May/June 2009 issue of the Harvard Education Letter.

CHAPTER 14

Reinforcement, Richness, and Relationships: The Three R's of One Model Afterschool Program

A Boston program looks beyond tutoring and homework help to build student success

Andreae Downs

Three well-scrubbed eighth graders sit around a conference table at the Richard J. Murphy School in Boston and politely explain why they come to Prime Time, the Murphy's afterschool program: homework help.

"My parents can't really help me; the work is new for them," says Gerald. If he couldn't go to Prime Time, he adds, "I'd be frustrated at home. It would be difficult for me to do my work."

Nick agrees: "All the teachers stay, so if you don't understand the assignment, you can go talk to the teacher that assigned it."

Stephanie says that if she went home to do homework she'd experience a lot more computer crashes, and she wouldn't have the library nearby.

But is homework help the *real* reason these students come to Prime Time?

"Well, it *is* fun," Stephanie finally admits. "Especially the dance classes and science experiments, or projects on ecosystems," she adds enthusiastically. Gerald likes "playing football with the boys, or basketball" on Fridays and "doing art" on Thursdays. Nick likes Destination ImagiNation(r), a creativity and problem-solving program whereby teachers step back from instruction while children solve a particular problem or create something new—projects ranging from a model rocket to a play.

All three students also say they like the people and the atmosphere at Prime Time. "One reason I like to be here is the first time I came, everyone was friendly—the teachers, the kids, everyone," Gerald says.

A COMPREHENSIVE APPROACH

Prime Time has been a central component of principal Mary Russo's efforts to improve academic achievement at the 950-student Murphy, Boston's largest K–8 public school, with remarkable results. When Russo arrived at the school in 1999, 58 percent of fourth graders failed the math portion of the Massachusetts Comprehensive Assessment System (MCAS), the state's standardized achievement test, and one in three could not read at grade level. In 2005, the Murphy's fourth graders had the third-highest MCAS scores in Boston, and more than 90 percent passed both the math and English/language arts portions of the test.

In addition, Russo herself has received statewide and national recognition as an instructional leader. In 2005, she was named one of five National Distinguished Principals by the National Association of Elementary School Principals, and she was named the 2004 Massachusetts Principal of the Year by Boston's After-School for All Partnership, a public–private

venture to promote high-quality before and afterschool programs in the city.

Russo is the first to admit that the Murphy's extensive afterschool program is not the only reason for her students' success. She cites the expansion of the school to a K–8 (from a
K–5), along with districtwide efforts to expand professional
development and improve math and language arts curricula,
as other keys to the school's turnaround. But the Murphy's
heavy emphasis on afterschool is clearly one factor that has
made it stand out as a local, state, and even national model.
And Russo believes that the secret of Prime Time's success
lies in the comprehensiveness of its approach to supporting
student success.

Those who visit Prime Time in the early afternoon will see
students receiving homework help in groups or one-on-one
tutoring. What they won't see is how focused the program is
on reinforcing the work students do during the regular school
day, and on building effective working relationships among
students and the Murphy faculty. Murphy teachers staff Prime
Time and maintain regular communication with each child's
daytime teachers. Tutors are either Murphy teachers or Murphy interns—the school makes extensive use of students in
local teacher-education programs—and afterschool program
director Jonna Casey shares Russo's office. School rules on behavior also apply in Prime Time.

Besides an hour or so of daily homework time and tutoring as needed, Prime Time gives students an opportunity to
participate in a variety of enrichment activities and includes a
strong arts component. The program offers instrumental music lessons, dance classes, a variety of clubs, and art instruction. Students interested in admission to the city's arts high
school can develop a portfolio. Prime Time also includes occasional field trips and special programs run by outside agencies like Historic New England, the nation's oldest and largest

regional preservation program. Facilitators from Historic New England bring in actual and re-created artifacts, explain their relevance to their former owners, and ask students to reflect on and respond to the works in art and in writing.

Prime Time also includes another enrichment component whereby students are introduced to adults representing a variety of different professions. Staff from the National Wildlife Federation, for instance, provide a six-week environmental unit, and volunteers from the Boston Society of Architects come to Prime Time and work with the children on design projects.

"This is time for children to capture the excitement of learning," says Russo. She adds that the program gives children many enrichment opportunities they might not otherwise have, and that these experiences can often spark a passion for learning that spills over into the school day.

Russo says the Murphy's Prime Time program also gives her and her afterschool faculty the opportunity to develop closer working relationships with parents. Because of budget constraints, there are no afterschool buses, so many parents come by the school to pick up their children.

"This is the happiest time of day for me. I can meet the parents, buttonhole them. It improves communication," Russo says.

And Russo and her students aren't the only fans of Prime Time. Richard Murnane, an economist at the Harvard Graduate School of Education who has recently conducted extensive research in the Boston Public Schools, says the kinds of skills developed in programs like Prime Time are among those most in demand in today's job market. These include creating a project to test a hypothesis, active listening, working with others, social skills, presentation skills, and knowing how to work with common computer programs. Standardized tests are incapable of measuring most of these skills, Murnane notes, yet they can be of tremendous value, particularly to low-income children who may otherwise have few opportunities to develop them.

BUILDING SUPPORT FOR AFTERSCHOOL

Russo has long been a champion of afterschool programs, since well before they were fashionable, she says. In 1990, Russo faced an uphill battle but ultimately succeeded in starting an afterschool program at the school she previously led, the Samuel W. Mason School in Boston's Roxbury neighborhood. The Mason was one of the least-selected schools in Boston's school choice program and was in danger of closing when Russo arrived. By 1997, the school was considered a model and was named a Blue Ribbon School of Excellence by the U.S. Department of Education and a Title 1 Distinguished School, in part because of its highly effective afterschool program.

The Mason's two-hour program, which employed both teachers and volunteers from the AmeriCorps youth program City Year, soon grew from its first two classes of 15 students each to a much larger afterschool program and six-week summer camp. In addition to its original focus on homework and literacy, the expanded program included a variety of enrichment opportunities as well as experimental instruction and curriculum.

By 1999, when Russo arrived at the Murphy, afterschool was an easier sell. She had the support of parents, community institutions, the mayor, and the school department to start a program that would be an integral part of the school's improvement effort. Other city departments had realized that youth crime peaked in the afterschool hours and had made more funds available for child care. In the meantime, Boston's service providers had moved toward a model of delivering the needed services within schools, and private funders such as the Nellie Mae Education Foundation had commissioned research that confirmed the academic and social benefits of quality programs outside of school hours.

"In 1990 the atmosphere for afterschool was discouraging, and we were out on a limb," Russo says, recalling how little financing was available and how some school officials disparaged a number of her ideas. "Now people are celebrated for doing afterschool."

ACCOUNTABILITY FOR AFTERSCHOOL

Afterschool programs have been in existence for about 130 years and have varied widely in format and intent, according to Robert Halpern, a professor at the Erikson Institute, a graduate school in child development and author of the book *Making Play Work: The Promise of After-School Programs for Low-Income Children*. As a result of the recent nationwide focus on standards and measurable academic achievement, afterschool has gotten additional attention and funding from both government and nonprofit sources, notes Crisanne L. Gayl, a researcher with the Progressive Policy Institute (see "Can Quality Out-of-School Programs Run on a Shoestring?"). In addition, afterschool has taken on a more academic focus in many schools, based on the notion that the programs offer children more time to hone their skills and raise their academic achievement—as well as their test scores.

But the nature of afterschool programs—that they are voluntary, attendance can be sporadic, and activities are not necessarily geared toward the development of specific academic skills—has meant that hard evidence linking afterschool programs to better test scores is slim, according to Gayl. The dearth of such evidence—and a 2003 Mathematica study of 21st Century Community Learning Center programs that showed no academic achievement gains at all—was cited by former education secretary Rod Paige as a reason to cut $400 million in federal afterschool funding in 2004. Congress ultimately held the funding steady, but the findings nonetheless raised questions for some about whether the government's investment in afterschool was yielding tangible returns.

What seems clearer from the research, however, is that students' attitudes about school and various academic-related behaviors, such as turning in homework and showing up for school regularly, are improved when students regularly attend a quality afterschool program. Beth Miller's 2003 review of the research on afterschool programs for the Nellie Mae Education Foundation noted that program participation was linked to several important factors: Children were more engaged in learning, finished homework more often and with more attention, had fewer absences, and had better relationships with adults and peers in their school environments.

Whether the Murphy's out-of-school programs, which also include a weekend test-prep program called Saturday Scholars and several summer programs, actually improve test scores and other academic outcomes has not been rigorously studied. Initial statistical analysis of the state achievement test indicates that none of the children who attend afterschool programs at the Murphy fall into the two lowest achievement categories. While school statisticians say it's unclear whether this is because of the additional attention and time students get in the afterschool program or because the students who enroll come from more motivated families, Russo clearly believes Prime Time makes the difference. "It's a kind of intervention [for lower-achieving students]," she says. "For these children, we would definitely recommend the afterschool program."

For children who need extra help—and even for those who don't—Prime Time is an incredible deal. The full fee for one student is $40 per year, $60 for two students or more from the same family. Afterschool programs in nearby suburbs can run $230 a month or more for the same number of hours. Private

CAN QUALITY OUT-OF-SCHOOL PROGRAMS RUN ON A SHOESTRING?

Mary Russo, principal at the Murphy School, says the funding her school receives from outside sources is only a part of what it takes to make the Murphy's out-of-school programs successful. In a recent interview with *HEL*, Russo discussed some of the other ways that school leaders—even those on shoestring budgets—can tap into existing school and community resources to help make out-of-school programming a reality:

- Take an "all-funds" approach to your budget. Lay out all the money available and look at it as one big pot of cash. Then set afterschool as a priority.
- Explore flexible scheduling for teachers—some may come in later and stay later, as we do with many of our middle school teachers.
- Explore contracting out with arts and music agencies in your community. Sometimes they will work for less than the teacher stipend.
- Look at agencies that offer free programs for schools. We use Boston's Parks and Recreation Department, the National Wildlife Federation, and others.
- Make your school community aware of grant opportunities out there. Here at the Murphy, we say, "No grant is too small; no grant is too big." All the teachers get involved in writing grants, and about 10 percent of our budget is raised through grants.
- Look at the resources you already have. Our school, for instance, is also a community center. That means that heat and electricity and custodians are already in the budget.

So look at what you can use to get started—it creates a better sense of how you can use resources other than money.

- The fact that you've established an afterschool program means that you are eligible for resources from organizations that want to help. Parents can be a valuable source of this kind of information.

tutoring in the Boston area starts at $35 per hour. But because so many of the Murphy's students qualify for free or reduced-price lunch (73 percent), the afterschool program is eligible for a variety of private and public funding sources, which the program's directors actively pursue for its $480,000 annual budget.

Yet even at 307 students, about a third of the school's student population, Russo is still not satisfied with the Murphy's afterschool programs and wants them to have a much broader reach. "We want all children [involved in the programs]," she says. "They could have more time to learn, they could do more cultural activities, instrumental music, second languages. We could add more value to their education with more time."

Russo says she could enroll more children if their parents could pick them up at the end of the day. Because of Boston's 30-year-old desegregation plan, students are bused across the city to the Murphy, but many parents are unable to pick up their children at the Murphy, either because they cannot make it to the school by the six-o'clock end time or they do not have a car.

Another issue that virtually every school with an afterschool program faces is the funding required for the extra teacher time, as well as maintaining instructional quality and preventing teacher burnout. Currently, many of the teachers who stay for Prime Time do so only a few days a week, since staying after school more often is difficult for teachers with a lot of additional responsibilities.

Despite these complications, however, Russo would like to see the program grow and hopes eventually to add many of the enrichment opportunities currently available in suburban schools to Prime Time. For one thing, she would like to add more sports so that students like Gerald could have more options. "We have a tremendous field here," Russo says. "I would love to offer lacrosse to our kids."

This chapter originally appeared in the March/April 2005 issue of the Harvard Education Letter.

FOR FURTHER READING

C. L. Gayl. "After-School Programs: Expanding Access and Ensuring Quality." Washington, DC: Progressive Policy Institute Policy Report, July 2004.

R. Halpern. *Making Play Work: The Promise of After-School Programs for Low-Income Children*. New York, NY: Teachers College Press, 2003.

T. Kane. "The Impact of After-School Programs." New York, NY: William T. Grant Foundation, January 2004. Available online at www.wtgrantfoundation.org

B. M. Miller. "Critical Hours: Afterschool Program and Educational Success." Quincy, MA: Nellie Mae Education Foundation, May 2003.

E. R. Reisner, R. N. White, C. A. Russell, and J. Birmingham. "Building Quality, Scale, and Effectiveness in After-School Programs." Washington, DC: Policy Studies Associates, Inc., November 2, 2004. Available online at www.policystudies.com

CHAPTER 15

Meeting of the Minds

The parent-teacher conference is the cornerstone of school-home relations. How can it work for all families?

Laura Pappano

A gnes Jackson isn't proud to admit it, but last year she didn't attend a single parent-teacher conference for her youngest son, who just completed third grade at the Thomas O'Brien Academy of Science and Technology in Albany, New York.

It's not as if she didn't try. Jackson did respond when the school asked her to select a time for a face-to-face meeting. "They asked me what time could I be there and I told them, but they said, 'Oh, somebody already took that,'" says Jackson, a single mother of three who works nights as a certified nursing assistant. She made several impromptu visits to the school, whose Web site touts it as a "nationally recognized Blue Ribbon School of Excellence," but each time her son's teacher was unavailable. "They'd say, 'You need to wait until school is over,'" she recalls.

The parent-teacher conference may be the most critical, yet awkward, ritual in the school calendar. It is treated as a key barometer of parental involvement, so important that a

Texas lawmaker in 2007 proposed fining parents $500 and charging them with a Class C misdemeanor for skipping one. New York City Mayor Michael R. Bloomberg wants to pay poor families up to $5,000 a year to meet goals, including attending parent-teacher conferences.

Yet, in practice, these conferences can be ill-defined encounters whose very high-pressure design—bringing together a child's two most powerful daily influences for sometimes super-brief meetings about academic and social progress—make them a volatile element in home-school relations. For schools, parent-teacher conferences can be a nightmare to organize and may leave teachers spinning after hours of quick encounters. For parents, sessions can feel more like speed dating than team building and may encourage snap judgments (see "Conference Do's and Don'ts").

Surveys of K–8 parent involvement conducted by the National Center for Educational Statistics indicate that a majority of parents attended parent-teacher conferences in 2003. Yet, many are still absent. Those parents who might most need to show often don't or can't. The most involved can now, in a growing number of districts, access their child's homework, grades, and attendance online.

Given the weight that parents and teachers place on these once- or twice-a-year get-togethers, what can schools do to ensure that parent-teacher conferences are effective and productive—and meet the needs of all families?

THE "TWO-WAY" CONFERENCE

Kathleen Hoover-Dempsey, associate professor and chair of the department of psychology and human development at Vanderbilt University, who studies home-school communication, says face-to-face conversations are more effective than written notes and e-mails, especially when the teacher has concerns or suggestions to make. For parents, "the heart just leaps a bit at

CONFERENCE DO'S AND DON'TS

Some teachers dread parent-teacher conferences because no one has taught them what to do—or what not to do, says Todd Whitaker, professor of educational leadership at Indiana State University and author or coauthor of several books, including *Dealing with Difficult Parents*.

His advice for setting a positive tone and dealing with difficult parents:

- Hold the first parent-teacher conference early in the year, before children get into trouble or fall behind. Call parents in advance if there is a problem. Nothing in the conference should be a surprise.
- Sit next to the person. "We are on the same team," says Whitaker.
- Even if parents are angry, keep calm and treat them in a positive manner.
- Speak about "we" and not "you": "What can we do together so your son can be more successful?"
- Focus on the future. Do not treat conferences as a conclusion but as a step along a path.

the thought that something is wrong," she says. Conferences should include a chance for parents to share observations or concerns, specifics from the teacher about positive things a child is doing, and thoughts on how the teacher and parent might support a child's performance, Hoover-Dempsey says.

Many schools are rethinking conferences to make them less a complaint session and more a collaborative discussion, she says. "People are really starting to talk about the 'two-way parent-teacher conference' and the 'mutually respectful parent-teacher conference.' The conference is not for me to give you my judgment, but for us to share experiences and suggestions about things we can do to really support this child's education."

Collaborative conferences can be promoted by "bundling" them with other chances for parents and teachers to communicate, according to Karen Mapp, lecturer at the Harvard Graduate School of Education and a coauthor of *Beyond the Bake Sale: The Essential Guide to Family-School Partnerships*. Very effective schools may hold several face-to-face conferences each year, including some in which students present their schoolwork and share responses to questions they have pondered in advance, says Mapp, former deputy superintendent for family and community engagement for the Boston Public Schools. Others may be times for parents and teachers to meet solo and discuss an agenda agreed upon in advance. The key, says Mapp, is that the school community should shape how conference time is used (see "Laying the Groundwork for Successful Parent-Teacher Conferences").

SHIFTING DYNAMICS: A LARGER ROLE FOR PARENTS

Building a two-way exchange, says Janet Chrispeels, professor of education studies at the University of California at San Diego, also requires shifting the dynamic of the conference from *reporting on* a child to *eliciting from* parents a better understanding of a child's strengths at home, in order to provide clues to helping them at school. Questions that might reveal these clues include:

- What homework habits does your child have that make you proud?
- In what ways is your child working up to his or her expectations?
- What things at school make your child happiest? Most upset?

- Think of a time when your child dealt with a difficult situation that made you very proud. What did you see as the strengths of your child in that situation?

Chrispeels, who trains teachers in conducting parent conferences, says such questions are important both for the information they provide teachers and because they position parents as partners in their child's schooling. The process also lets parents know that teachers realize children may be acting differently at school than at home.

Teachers should be prepared to show concrete examples of academic expectations, including student papers with names removed. "Teachers need to be able to explain to parents, 'Here is the range of work in this class,'" says Chrispeels. That way, she says, parents can have a better idea of what the teacher will be encouraging students to achieve in the future.

Chrispeels advocates ending conferences with what she calls a "one to grow on" message, to let parents know what the teacher intends to do to address any areas of weakness—and how the parent might help at home. Sometimes that can be as simple as explaining what skills they are working on in school and what resources are available to help students outside of school, like a before-school phonics help session.

Even parents of children who are doing well in school need reassurance that their child is developmentally, socially, and intellectually on track, says Chrispeels. Teachers also have experience and information to relay, for example, about planning high school course loads to meet graduation and college-entrance requirements. This helps parents anticipate a child's stresses and needs.

FACILITATING PARTICIPATION

More parent-teacher dialogue means schools must work harder to meet parents on their turf and tailor meetings to

LAYING THE GROUNDWORK FOR SUCCESSFUL PARENT-TEACHER CONFERENCES

To foster parent-teacher talk—formal or informal—Claire Crane, principal of the Robert L. Ford School in Lynn, Mass., has structured her school to get parents in the building as often as she can. Many are recent immigrants working two or three jobs, so she lures them to school by meeting *their* needs. School is open Monday and Tuesday until 9 p.m., when 250 parents attend English as a Second Language classes and a course on surviving in the United States. Ford staff members teach the classes and provide babysitting and a chance to connect.

The school also operates like a community center. Parents perform in neighborhood talent shows, raise money, and plant trees to beautify the grounds. They have even volunteered alongside city health officials to try to halt a rat problem by putting out bait.

Crane says the intense level of involvement and communication enhances parent-teacher relationships and, in turn, both the formal and informal conferences that take place. So when it's time for formal parent-teacher conference nights three times a year, Crane says, "I can't handle the crowds."

As a result, when there are difficult conversations to have—and there are plenty in a school in which one-third of students attend summer school in order to be promoted—parents feel they are on the same team with the school.

"I feel so much confidence in the principal, I come and ask her, 'What can I do?'" says Beverly Ellis, a mother of five and Ford School parent for 22 years. Ellis, who has two children at the school now, recently had to speak with teachers when her daughter started throwing erasers in her sixth-grade class. "I like to hear they are doing good. But if things are not going right, you can talk to the teachers."

suit particular lifestyles and needs. Because their parent populations can vary significantly, school administrators are using different approaches to facilitate parent-teacher conferencing.

At Arlington (Mass.) High School, an upper-middle-class suburb of Boston where 72 percent of graduates go on to four-year colleges, parents can now sign up online for five-minute, face-to-face parent-teacher conferences. It's so popular that when administrators opened up the conference registration at midnight in the fall of 2004, 200 slots were booked in the first 10 minutes. Principal Charles Skidmore says online registration gives parents more choice and control, and, as a result, teachers are drawing more parents to conferences. "We are seeing some of the 'hard-to-reach' parents," Skidmore reports.

The situation is much different at the K–8 Robert L. Ford School in Lynn, Mass., where 90 percent of students are low-income and 58.5 percent speak English as a second language. Principal Claire Crane has created multiple ways for parents and teachers to talk, including holding parent-teacher conferences as early as 7 a.m. and as late as 9 p.m. These conferences are sensitive to parents' needs. They are folded into family evenings that include displays of student work (no babysitters needed, and kids can show off learning). There is food. There are translators. The conferences are never held in the winter (easier for families with babies). Last year, Crane even held a conference in the street because a father with health problems couldn't easily get out of his car.

The formula appears to have worked. Crane, whose school has an attendance rate of 95.5 percent, had 92 percent of families come to an open house in November 2006 and attend parent-teacher conferences later that same night.

Other schools focus on welcoming parents during the school day. At Harriet Gibbons High School in Albany, N.Y., a school serving ninth graders in a community in which 40 percent of students qualify for free or reduced-priced lunches, principal

Anthony Clement built parent-teacher conference time into the daily school schedule. Team A teachers are available from 12:40 p.m. to 1:40 p.m., and Team B teachers are available from 10:30 a.m. to 11:30 a.m. If parents are not free during the conference hour, teachers will meet at other times, or—as in the case of the mother of a child in math teacher George Benson's class who must pack up three young kids and take two city buses to attend a conference—plan regular phone calls. School social workers will even make home visits. Noting that many of his parents work at jobs with hourly wages, Clement says, "We know when a parent is here, we need to see them."

As a result, Clement says, 80 percent of parents have attended one or two daytime parent-teacher conferences *in addition* to the two districtwide conferences held on two school days in November and January. Clement credits the emphasis on conferencing with increasing school attendance from 63 percent last year to 85 percent this year, more parent involvement in school activities, and a dramatic uptick in ninth graders earning five or more of the required credits for promotion to tenth grade, from 45 percent last year to almost 70 percent this year.

The school's approach has also helped parents like Agnes Jackson get involved in her middle son's education. Where Jackson has yet to attend a conference at her third grader's school, she sat down more than a dozen times with her ninth-grade son's teachers at Harriet Gibbons—and that doesn't count scores of informal conversations about her son's school progress.

The frequent conferences have given Jackson a better handle on how the school system works and what is expected of her children. "In the past, I was quick to say, 'These people are doing this to my child,'" she says. "Now I ask, 'But what is my child doing that causes this to happen?' I can hear good and bad. But it's all good because I know how to respond to help my child. It helps me to say, 'OK, bud, you've got to do this,'" says Jackson. "It's helped me to grow as a single parent."

The easy access to teachers at Harriet Gibbons has also colored her views about her son's schools. Her third grader's school, she says, "will call if there is a problem," whereas the constant conversation with her ninth grader's teachers has made her more of a partner. "They tell me about his potential; they tell me what he is capable of doing," she says.

This chapter originally appeared in the July/August 2007 issue of the Harvard Education Letter.

FOR FURTHER READING

A. T. Henderson, K. L. Mapp, V. R. Johnson, and D. Davies. *Beyond the Bake Sale: The Essential Guide to Family-School Partnerships*. New York, NY: New Press, 2007.

K. V. Hoover-Dempsey and J. M. T. Walker. "Family-School Communication." Paper prepared for Research Committee of the Metropolitan Nashville/Davidson County Board of Public Education, March 2002.

S. Lawrence-Lightfoot. *The Essential Conversation: What Parents and Teachers Can Learn from Each Other*. New York, NY: Random House, 2003.

About the Contributors

Michael Bitz is the founder of the Comic Book Project and co-founder of the Youth Music Exchange. The first recipient of the Educational Entrepreneurship Fellowship at the Mind Trust in Indianapolis, he also received the Distinguished Alumni Early Career Award from Teachers College, Columbia University. Dr. Bitz has served on the faculties at Teachers College, Columbia University; and Ramapo College.

Mitch Bogen is an education writer based in Somerville, Mass.

Caroline T. Chauncey is the editor of the *Harvard Education Letter* and assistant director of Harvard Education Publishing Group.

Andreae Downs is a freelance education writer in Newton, Mass.

James Paul Gee is Mary Lou Fulton Presidential Professor of Literacy Studies at Arizona State University and the author of numerous articles in sociolinguistics, literacy studies, cognitive science, and discourse analysis. He is the author of *What Video Games Have to Teach Us about Learning and Literacy* (Palgrave Macmillan).

Colleen Gillard is an education writer based in Cambridge, Mass.

Sam M. Intrator is associate professor of education and the Program in Urban Studies at Smith College and codirector of the Urban Educational Initiative, which places Smith students in urban classrooms with the goal of encouraging them to learn about the theoretical, practical, and human issues facing urban youth and city schools. He is the author of *Leading from Within: Poetry That Sustains the Courage to Lead* (Jossey-Bass).

Michael J. Nakkula is a practice professor at the University of Pennsylvania Graduate School of Education. He was previously a research associate at the Harvard Graduate School of Education, where he taught courses on counseling, urban education, and adolescent development. He is coauthor, with Eric Toshalis, of *Understanding Youth: Adolescent Development for Educators* (Harvard Education Press).

Pedro A. Noguera is a professor in the Steinhardt School of Culture, Education, and Human Development at New York University. He is also executive director of the Metropolitan Center for Urban Education and codirector of the Institute for the Study of Globalization and Education in Metropolitan Settings (IGEMS).

Laura Pappano writes about education and is writer-in-residence at the Wellesley Centers for Women at Wellesley College. She is coauthor, with Eileen McDonagh, of *Playing with the Boys: Why Separate Is Not Equal in Sports* (Oxford University Press).

George Sugai is professor of special education in the Neag School of Education at the University of Connecticut. He is also codirector of the Center of Positive Behavioral Interventions and Supports (PBIS).

Eric Toshalis is assistant professor of education at California State University, Channel Islands. He is coauthor, with Michael J. Nakkula, of *Understanding Youth: Adolescent Development for Educators* (Harvard Education Press).

Nancy Walser is the assistant editor of the *Harvard Education Letter*. A former newspaper journalist, Walser served eight years on the Cambridge, Mass., School Committee. She is currently a master's student at the Harvard Graduate School of Education and is author of the forthcoming book, *The Essential School Board Book:*

Better Governance in the Age of Accountability (Harvard Education Press).

Richard Weissbourd is a lecturer in education at the Harvard Graduate School of Education and the Kennedy School of Government. He is a founder of several children's initiatives, including ReadBoston, WriteBoston, and the Lee Academy Pilot School.

David McKay Wilson is a freelance education journalist based in New York State.

DATE DUE

UFOs

AND OTHER CLOSE ENCOUNTERS

by Neil Nixon

illustrated by David A. Hardy

Ladybird

Contents

Acknowledgments

The author and publishers wish to thank the following for permission to use copyright material:
Page 11 (bottom): Aetherius Society; pages 34/35: Aviation Photos International;
pages 17 (top), 19, 45: Mary Evans Picture Library; page 15: Fortean Picture Library;
page 35: Getty Images; pages 18, 31: Images Colour Library and Philip Daly;
page 29: The Kobal Collection and "Close Encounters of the Third Kind";
page 22: LWT, "Strange But True"; page 40: Mirror Syndication;
pages 6, 8(3), 11 (top), 16, 26: Paul Popper Ltd;
page 27: Science Photo Library and Jack Finch; page 17 (bottom): "UFO Reality" and Steve Holt.

Introduction

The universe is the name given to all of space. Space includes our own planet, the Earth, and countless other stars and planets. There are many mysteries about the universe.

Mysteries are things we don't understand. Mystery stories are popular because they excite people and make them think about the answers.

This book looks at mysteries of Earth and space. There are many different kinds of mysteries: about people, about places, and about things.

The universe includes Earth and all of space

Mystery stories interest everyone

The universe

The universe itself is a mystery. People who study stars and planets—called **astronomers**—have found out many things. But they still don't know the age of the universe, or how large it is. They also disagree about how it was formed.

The sun

The sun is a star. It has nine **planets** around it, all of different sizes. They also have years of different lengths. A year is the time it takes for a planet to go around the sun. Going around the sun in this way is called **orbiting**.

All the planets spin around. When a planet has spun around completely it has completed one day. Each planet has a different length of day.

Big bang

One idea was advanced in 1930 by Belgian astronomer Georges Lemaitre. He suggested that about 10 billion years ago our universe was formed in a "big bang". He thought that one single lump of matter exploded at that time to make everything we can see today.

Some other astronomers disagree, and think the universe has always been here.

Solar system mysteries

A solar system is a star with a group of planets. The sun is at the center of our own solar system. Although we know a lot about the planets, there are still many mysteries connected with our solar system. Here are just four:

- How old is it?
- Are there any more planets waiting to be discovered?
- Was there once another planet that has now broken up?
- Is Earth the only planet with life?

So far, no one has definite answers to these questions.

The sun

There is still a lot to find out about the sun. By launching telescopes and satellites into space we are finding out more all the time. This photograph, taken from a space station, shows bright spots on the sun's surface. There are strange flares, dark spots, and other mysteries about the sun still to be solved.

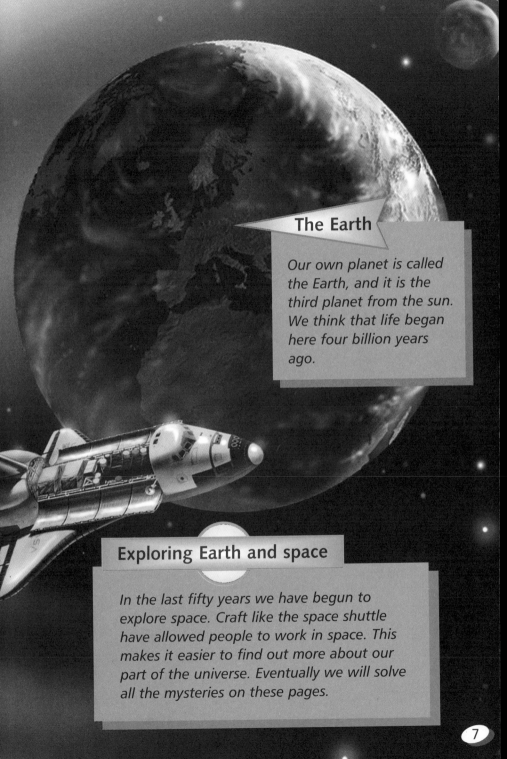

The Earth

Our own planet is called the Earth, and it is the third planet from the sun. We think that life began here four billion years ago.

Exploring Earth and space

In the last fifty years we have begun to explore space. Craft like the space shuttle have allowed people to work in space. This makes it easier to find out more about our part of the universe. Eventually we will solve all the mysteries on these pages.

Our mysterious satellite

Besides Earth, the only place in the solar system that has been explored by people is the moon. At 10:56 p.m. (Florida Time) on July 20, 1969, Neil Armstrong became the first person to set foot on the moon. So far, twelve people have walked on its surface.

A Saturn 5 rocket blasts off, taking men to the moon.

Edwin Aldrin, second man on the moon, comes down to the surface to start collecting rocks.

Old rocks

The first moon rocks to be collected were three billion years old—much older than had been expected. One rock proved to be 4.6 billion years old, older than any rock ever found on Earth.

Old mysteries, new mysteries

American **astronauts** went to the moon six times between 1969 and 1972. When the missions began, people wondered about the age of the moon, and what kind of rock it is made of. But some of the answers gathered by the astronauts led to even more mysteries.

Moon questions

Today, scientists wonder where the moon came from. If it is much older than Earth, it may have existed in space before the Earth was formed.

9

Mystery of life

We know there is life on Earth, but are we alone in space?
Over the years many people have reported meeting creatures from other worlds, known as **aliens**.

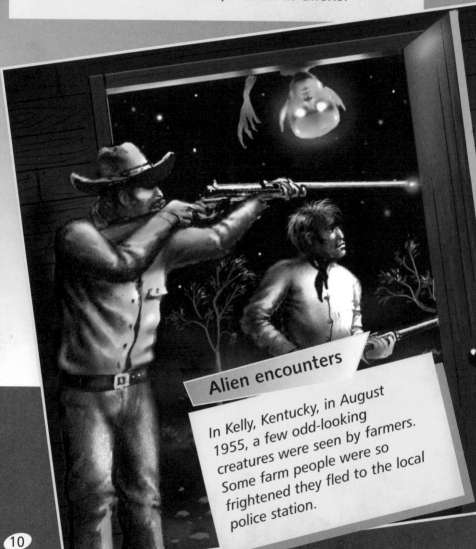

Alien encounters

In Kelly, Kentucky, in August 1955, a few odd-looking creatures were seen by farmers. Some farm people were so frightened they fled to the local police station.

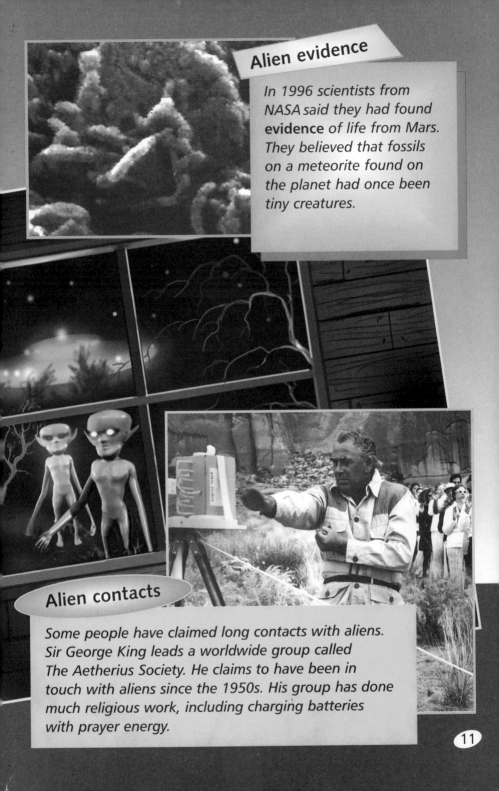

Alien evidence

In 1996 scientists from NASA said they had found **evidence** of life from Mars. They believed that fossils on a meteorite found on the planet had once been tiny creatures.

Alien contacts

Some people have claimed long contacts with aliens. Sir George King leads a worldwide group called The Aetherius Society. He claims to have been in touch with aliens since the 1950s. His group has done much religious work, including charging batteries with prayer energy.

Encounters in space

Some people suggest that we have already found life in space. Many others believe that this isn't true. Here are some claims and possible explanations.

Lights in space

This is a meteor burning up as it enters Earth's atmosphere. There are many small objects in space, most of them unknown. They can cause lights in the sky. Sometimes they can look like craft when the sun shines on them in space.

Men on the moon

Some people claim they can see evidence on photographs of life in space. There are claims that this picture of the moon shows a dome on the surface. It is more likely to have been a fault in printing.

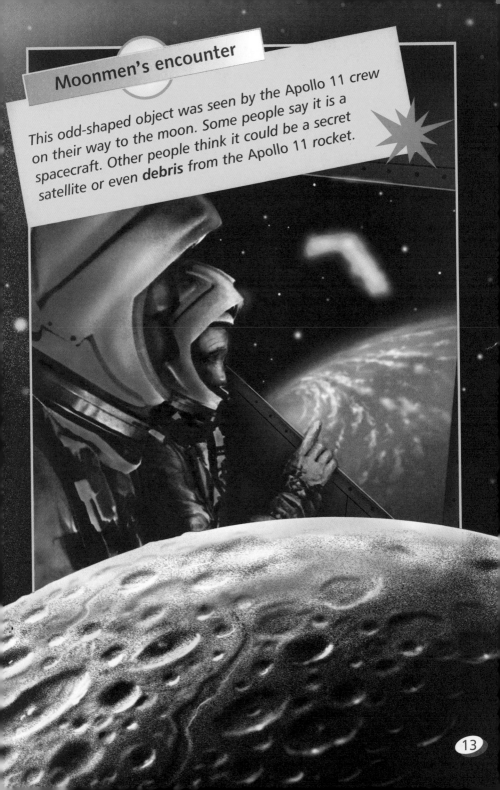

Moonmen's encounter

This odd-shaped object was seen by the Apollo 11 crew on their way to the moon. Some people say it is a spacecraft. Other people think it could be a secret satellite or even **debris** from the Apollo 11 rocket.

13

The UFO mysteries

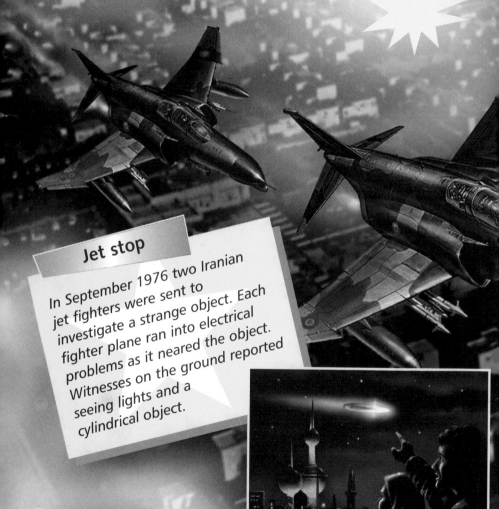

Many people have reported sightings of **UFOs** — unidentified flying objects. Sightings of UFOs are reported more often than meetings with aliens. Some people believe they are craft from other worlds.

Jet stop

In September 1976 two Iranian jet fighters were sent to investigate a strange object. Each fighter plane ran into electrical problems as it neared the object. Witnesses on the ground reported seeing lights and a cylindrical object.

Light over Paris

This photograph was taken in Paris in 1953 by an engineer called Paul Paulin. He saw a strange object over the city. The photograph shows that the object moved and then stopped in the air. This is something a plane couldn't do.

Close encounters of the first kind

There have been so many encounters with UFOs and their occupants that a famous researcher called J. Allen Hynek began to classify the different kinds. In a close encounter of the first kind (CE1) witnesses see an object they can't explain.

A puzzling photograph

On May 11, 1950, an object flew over a farm in Oregon. Farmer Paul Trent and his wife watched it and took two photographs. These have been carefully investigated, and no evidence of trickery has been found.

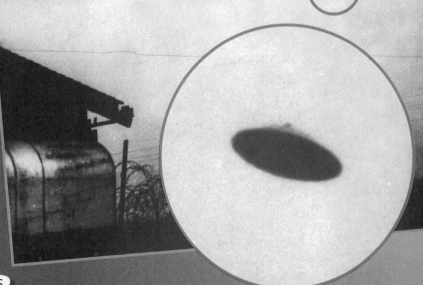

The problem with photographs

This photograph which was taken by a deputy sheriff in Minnesota, is typical of many CE1 cases. It is a mystery, but since nothing in the photograph suggests the size of the object, this mystery will probably never be solved.

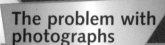

Flying triangles

This is a computer re-creation of an object seen in Lancashire, England, in 1996. Many similar objects have been seen in Europe and the U.S.A. One theory is that they are aircraft being tested in secret.

Close encounters of the second kind

In a close encounter of the second kind (CE2), witnesses see a UFO or alien at close range, and there is some trace of the event left behind. This trace might be left at the site. It could also be something picked up by a witness or even something that happens to the witness. Some interesting cases occurred in Canada and the U.S.A. in the 1960s.

Peculiar pancakes

American farmer Joe Simonton saw a strange craft hovering near his yard in 1961. Three small dark-haired men were inside, and they gave the farmer three pancakes. Simonton ate one and said it tasted "like cardboard". The remaining pancakes were later analyzed and proved to be ordinary pancakes without salt. Simonton was thought to be an honest man, and this strange UFO mystery has never been solved.

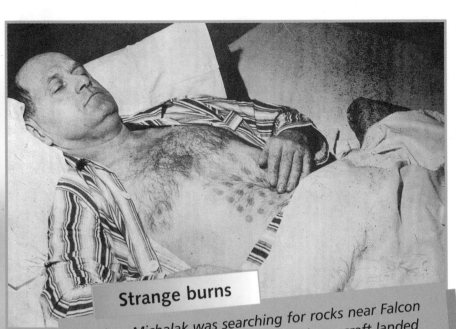

Strange burns

Stephen Michalak was searching for rocks near Falcon Lake, Canada, in May 1967 when a large craft landed nearby. He watched it through his protective goggles as it changed color. When he went forward to speak to anyone inside, a hatch closed and the craft took off, blasting Michalak with hot gas. He was later treated for burns to his chest. The strange pattern of the burns matched his description of the grille that let out the gas.

Socorro saucer

This strange craft was seen by a policeman at Socorro, New Mexico, in April 1964. Two silver-suited figures appeared near the craft, which took off with a loud roar. The feet of the craft left imprints in the ground, and some of the surrounding plants caught fire as it took off.

Close encounters of the third kind

In a close encounter of the third kind (CE3), witnesses view a craft at close range and see some living creatures. These encounters are fairly rare but often become well known because they are so spectacular.

African encounter

In Mutare, Zimbabwe, in August 1981, Clifford Muchena saw a bright light move across a lawn and hit a tower. He also saw two silver-suited beings who appeared to glow with light. Other people in the area saw the same things.

The Grays

In recent years the most common type of creature reported in sightings of UFOs has been the "Gray". Grays are said to be up to 4 feet tall with large heads and thin arms and legs.

Giants in the park

In October 1989, a craft landed in a park in Voronezh, Russia. At least two giant creatures got out and wandered around. Investigators later found an area of flattened grass and four holes in the earth, thought to have been left by the legs of the craft.

The best close encounters

Some UFO cases are so well known that investigators think they will eventually prove that UFOs and aliens are real. Here are two of the most famous.

Rendlesham Forest, England, 1980

After Christmas in 1980, men at an American air base in England saw strange lights moving in a forest at the end of a runway. Some have since claimed that they had seen a craft moving through the trees, and a tape recording of the event has been released.

Roswell, New Mexico, 1947

In July 1947, something crashed into the desert near Roswell, New Mexico. American Air Force personnel removed the debris, and the press were told that a "flying disk" had crashed. Soon afterward the Air Force changed the story to suggest that a weather balloon had crashed. Since 1947, however, many witnesses have come forward to suggest that an alien spacecraft crashed near Roswell.

A British television reconstruction of the event in Rendlesham Forest.

Roswell evidence

Major Jesse Marcel with some of the evidence at Roswell, 1947.

23

Military encounters

Some UFO cases can possibly be explained away as secret military tests of new equipment, and there is some good evidence to support this idea. The countries that test most military equipment often generate the greatest number of UFO reports.

Radar UFO

Many UFOs show up on radar and appear to do things impossible for normal aircraft. In 1975 U.S. Air Force radar picked up a target that vanished in seconds—a feat impossible for any plane at that time.

Later it was admitted that a Stealth aircraft had been testing equipment that made it invisible to radar.

Such tests are often kept secret, even when they lead to UFO reports.

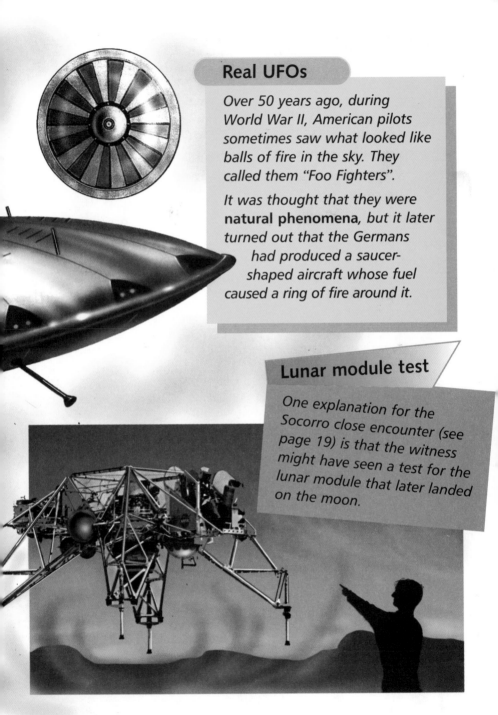

Real UFOs

Over 50 years ago, during World War II, American pilots sometimes saw what looked like balls of fire in the sky. They called them "Foo Fighters".

It was thought that they were **natural phenomena**, but it later turned out that the Germans had produced a saucer-shaped aircraft whose fuel caused a ring of fire around it.

Lunar module test

One explanation for the Socorro close encounter (see page 19) is that the witness might have seen a test for the lunar module that later landed on the moon.

Natural explanations

Occasionally, sightings of UFOs can be explained away as natural phenomena, like mistaken sightings of clouds. Some natural phenomena, like **earthlights**, are still being investigated, since no one knows quite what they are. Earthlights have been seen in laboratories, and above the ground.

Strange clouds

This strange cloud formation was photographed in New Zealand. Other cloud formations can appear to glow when seen in particular conditions. Some UFO reports come from people who see strange clouds.

Aurora Borealis/ Aurora Australis

These lights can be seen near the North and South Poles. They are caused by particles from space coming toward the Earth. They usually appear as bands of light but are sometimes seen as rapid flashes and moving lights.

Earthlights

Strange lights are sometimes seen floating in the air. The Hessdalen Valley in Norway had so many lights like this that researchers stayed out in freezing temperatures to investigate. They gathered some good photographs. Sometimes the lights appeared to change their pattern of flashing when laser beams were pointed at them.

The media

The **media** are the ways in which we get entertainment, information, and advice. They include newspapers, books, films, and magazines. Many things made by the media—like this book—deal with mysteries of Earth and space. Some people think that ideas from the media may lead people to expect to see UFOs and other strange things.

Men from Mars

Stories dealing with alien life have always been popular. In the early years of the 20th century many people thought that life on Mars might be like life on Earth.

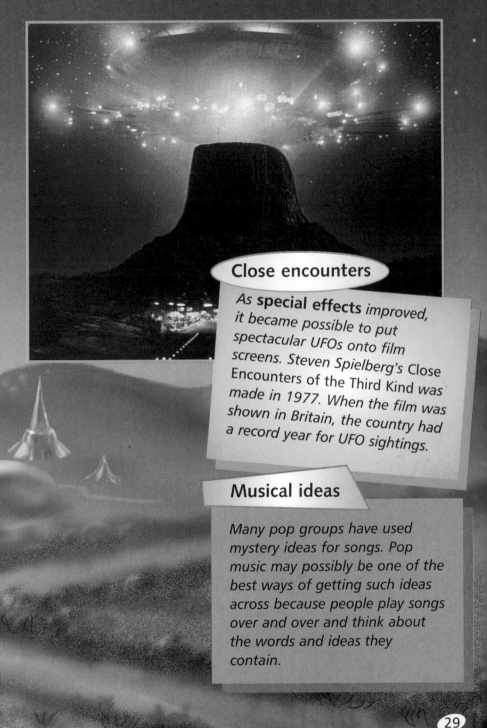

Close encounters

As **special effects** improved, it became possible to put spectacular UFOs onto film screens. Steven Spielberg's Close Encounters of the Third Kind was made in 1977. When the film was shown in Britain, the country had a record year for UFO sightings.

Musical ideas

Many pop groups have used mystery ideas for songs. Pop music may possibly be one of the best ways of getting such ideas across because people play songs over and over and think about the words and ideas they contain.

Historical mysteries

Throughout time all sorts of mysteries have been reported. Since the only records are old books, papers, and drawings, the causes of some of these reports can only be guessed at. In other cases the mysteries that were investigated led to important discoveries.

Changing thinking

Galileo Galilei (1564–1642) was an Italian mathematician, astronomer, and scientist. He helped develop the telescope. At the time people thought the sun went around the Earth. Galileo's observations of space didn't support this, and he was able to prove that the Earth goes around the sun.

Strange globes

This old woodcut shows an event in 1566 when people in the Swiss town of Basel saw "strange black and red globes" moving in the sky.

Strange lines

In the Peruvian desert near Nazca there is a 200-square-mile area of lines and animal carvings. These can be seen clearly from the air. They may be eight thousand years old. Recently, it has been suggested that the Indians who made the lines were able to fly using primitive hot-air balloons.

Mysterious places

Many mysteries are linked to particular places. Some place mysteries are legends–that is, stories passed down through history. The stories have changed so much over time that it may now be hard to find the original facts. Other mysteries occur because we don't know all the facts about places like Mars. Some are mysteries because, although we have the facts about a particular place, we find these facts hard to explain.

Atlantis

The Greek philosopher Plato wrote about an island that had vanished beneath the sea. Because many other stories include the same details, it seems likely that there was such a place. Over two thousand books have been written on this mystery, and more than a hundred places have been suggested as possible sites for Atlantis.

The Bermuda Triangle

Many ships and planes have disappeared in a triangular area of the Atlantic Ocean, near the island of Bermuda. Some people claim a strange force has caused these events, others think storms and fast currents are to blame. On December 5, 1945, five U.S. Navy aircraft and 14 men vanished without a trace.

The face on Mars

In June 1976 the unmanned space probe Viking 1 photographed the surface of Mars. One feature on the surface looked like a massive face carved into a rock in the Cydonia region of the planet. The face on Mars is almost one and a quarter miles long. It may be the result of erosion by storms.

Earth mysteries

Some people think that strange powers exist within the Earth and the atmosphere. They also think that people of the past understood more about these powers than we do today.

Strange stones

Throughout the world there are standing stones erected by ancient civilizations. Many are in Europe. Some investigators believe that the stones are linked with energy from the Earth. They also think that ancient sites occur along straight lines, known as **ley lines**.

Crop circles

By the late 1980s crop circles were common in Europe, many with complicated designs. Odd lights and sounds were reported in the same areas, and one video showed a small light bobbing about in a field near a crop circle.

Face in the clouds

This picture was taken from a bomber plane flying over Korea. After the photo was printed people noticed that the gaps in the clouds seemed to show the face of Jesus.

War of the worlds?

If there are aliens waiting to contact us, how will we first get in touch? Different people have different ideas.

Radio

*Scientists think that the most likely first contact will be a signal, probably by radio. A worldwide program called **SETI** is trying to find such a message.*

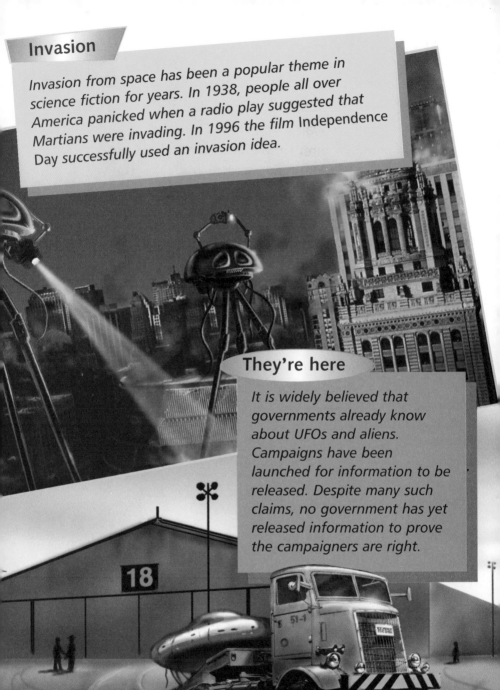

Invasion

Invasion from space has been a popular theme in science fiction for years. In 1938, people all over America panicked when a radio play suggested that Martians were invading. In 1996 the film Independence Day successfully used an invasion idea.

They're here

It is widely believed that governments already know about UFOs and aliens. Campaigns have been launched for information to be released. Despite many such claims, no government has yet released information to prove the campaigners are right.

18

51-1

Hoaxes

One problem with research into mysteries of Earth and space is that claims have been made that are not true. These claims are known as **hoaxes**. Over the years there have been many famous mystery hoaxes.

Doug and Dave

In 1991 two Englishmen, Dave Chorley and Doug Bower, confessed to making hundreds of crop circles. They showed a newspaper how they worked and produced one last circle that fooled a famous researcher. Many investigators now think that most of the complicated circles are fakes.

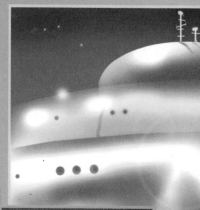

Pictures

Computer equipment now creates images that can look very real. This picture of UFOs over the Houses of Parliament in London was created using computer technology.

Girlfriend from space

Some people have written best-selling stories about their own experiences. In the 1950s a man called Truman Bethurum described romantic adventures with a woman called Aura Rhanes who was captain of a flying saucer. Most people believe he made up the story.

Strange cases

This book has looked at many of the most common kinds of reported Earth and space mysteries. Some cases are so strange they are almost impossible to explain.

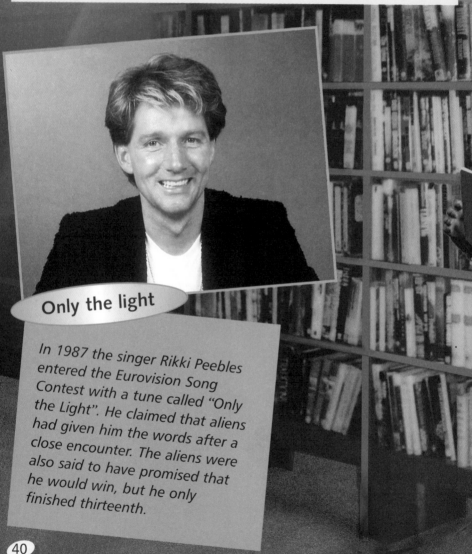

Only the light

In 1987 the singer Rikki Peebles entered the Eurovision Song Contest with a tune called "Only the Light". He claimed that aliens had given him the words after a close encounter. The aliens were also said to have promised that he would win, but he only finished thirteenth.

Bookshop encounter

Communion *is a best-selling book describing contact between an American author and "Gray" beings. In 1987 a man in a New York bookstore heard two people complaining about mistakes in the book. When he tried to speak to them, he realized they were "Gray" aliens!*

Finding answers

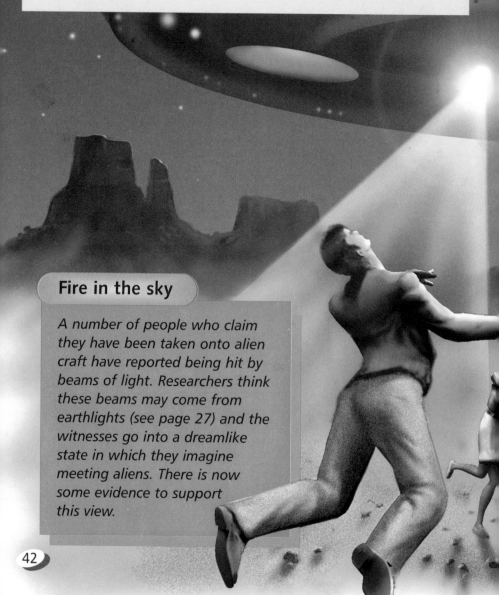

Today, mysteries of Earth and space are more popular than ever. Many investigators, often with different ideas, are adding their own answers as they find them.

Fire in the sky

A number of people who claim they have been taken onto alien craft have reported being hit by beams of light. Researchers think these beams may come from earthlights (see page 27) and the witnesses go into a dreamlike state in which they imagine meeting aliens. There is now some evidence to support this view.

Meeting and talking

There are many UFO conferences that allow researchers to gather together and discuss mysteries. Sharing ideas and information can lead to finding answers.

More evidence

There are more people than ever before with cameras and camcorders. This means more pictures and more evidence can be gathered about mysteries. This all helps in finding solutions.

What now?

History has taught us that solutions to mysteries often come over time. A new scientific discovery can sometimes suddenly explain old mysteries. New mysteries are always appearing, so we are not likely to run out.

Reaching for the stars

In the 21st century, we will probably travel farther and see deeper into space than ever before. We will certainly learn a lot.

And into the ground

In the 21st century, use of x-rays and electronic imaging equipment should allow us to investigate ancient sites without digging them up and damaging evidence.

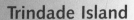

Trindade Island

This picture was taken in Brazil in 1958, and it has always puzzled investigators. The saucer-shaped object appears to be fuzzy. New discoveries in atmospheric research suggest it may be a rare natural phenomenon.

Amazing facts about UFOs

At least three American presidents have admitted seeing UFOs.

Earthlights have been seen near the sites of some stone circles and standing stones.

Ice circles, looking very much like crop circles, have been reported around the world.

Most people think of UFOs as massive. Some have been reported as small as an inch across.

A few researchers think the moon is a giant spaceship placed in orbit around the Earth.

There are people who believe that the moon missions never took place, and that all the films and photographs were made on Earth.

A British newspaper once invited teams to take part in a crop circle hoaxing competition.

In 1996 an insurance company in Great Britain said that a man calling himself Joseph Carpenter would be paid one million pounds after proving that he had been abducted by aliens. Many people were suspicious and it was soon proved that the story was made up to advertise insurance policies. Joseph Carpenter turned out to be a man with connections to the insurance company!

There have been some reports of attempted dog abductions. In one case in 1952 witnesses reported humanlike aliens making a pathetic attempt to kidnap a dog before heading back into their spaceship by walking right through the walls!

It is possible to get insurance against being taken aboard a UFO. So far a few thousand people have taken out policies.

Some scientists think that the asteroid belt between Mars and Jupiter is the remains of an old planet from our solar system.

Some people use the phrase "little green men" when they talk about aliens. In fact, very few reports of alien creatures describe them as green.

Some people have claimed that the face on Mars is in fact a giant statue of Elvis Presley.

In one of the strangest UFO cases in history a man from Brazil claimed he was taken aboard a UFO in 1969. He met hairy dwarflike creatures and noticed that there were stone walls inside the UFO!

UFO is only one of the terms used to describe strange flying objects. In the past the phrase "flying saucer" was more common. Some people prefer the term UAO (unidentified aerial object).

Glossary

Alien Creature from another world.

Astronaut Someone who travels in space.

Astronomer Person who studies space.

Debris Pieces of something larger that has broken up.

Earthlights Natural lights seen in the atmosphere.

Evidence Information that supports an argument.

Hoax A false claim about something.

Ley lines Thought to be straight lines linking ancient sites of power, such as stone circles.

Media Ways in which we use technology to communicate: radio, television, newspapers, books, the Internet, etc.

Natural phenomena Things that occur naturally.

Orbit To go around something. Satellites orbit the Earth.

Planet Large body in space that goes around a star. The Earth is a planet.

Rendlesham Forest Forest in Great Britain, scene of a famous UFO event.

Roswell Town in New Mexico. Near the site famous for a UFO event in July 1947.

SETI (Search for Extra-Terrestrial Intelligence) Scientific program searching for life in space.

Special effects Extra things added to films, television programs, etc., to make them more realistic and exciting.

UFO Unidentified flying object.